THE 5-HOUR SCHOOL WEEK

THE

5

HOUR

SCHOOL

WEEK

An Inspirational Guide
to Leaving the Classroom to
Embrace Learning in a Way
You Never Imagined

**AARON AND KALEENA
AMUCHASTEGUI**

LIONCREST
PUBLISHING

THE 5-HOUR SCHOOL WEEK
An Inspirational Guide to Leaving the Classroom to
Embrace Learning in a Way You Never Imagined

ISBN 978-1-5445-1225-9 *Paperback*
       978-1-5445-1224-2 *Ebook*

To the four coolest little humans we know! You are our greatest adventure! Your passion and creativeness inspire us daily. We love you more, always.

CONTENTS

PREFACE

Whenever you find yourself on the side of the majority, it is time to pause and reflect.

—MARK TWAIN

Hello, Fellow Parents:

The 5-Hour School Week was a solution to our family's biggest problem: the lack of time we had to live out our passions, create memories, and learn the stuff we felt was crucial for our kids to have a happy, healthy, successful life.

We are the parents of four incredible little humans: Madelyn, Charlotte, Isabel, and Brax. Married for twelve years, both Aaron and I are entrepreneurial by nature and the owners of several businesses that, luckily, continue to pay the bills. This book is a true collaboration between us but, for the sake of simplicity, is written in the first-person singular. However, at least half of the credit goes to my amazing husband, Aaron, who continues to inspire, support, and challenge me to grow every single day.

You will read about the way our life used to be and how we made the change to start living a life we didn't know was possible. I completely respect that not everyone dreams of traveling the world with their kids. Maybe your dream is running a local family farm, or having your kids participate in the business you already have. Maybe you are passionate about teaching your kids to sew, or paint, or design websites. Whether on the road or in your home, the 5-Hour School Week will free up precious hours in your kids' life to explore what they are truly passionate about and spend more time with the people who matter most—YOU!

The 5-Hour School Week works in two parts: first is the one to two hours of focused, concentrated learning. This time covers the topics of math, reading, writing, history, and so on. I guarantee that your kids can accomplish as much, if not more, in one hour of focused learning, compared to the seven hours they would spend at school, and retain what they learn. The second part is to explore whatever your heart desires! This is the best part! If you have a kid interested in coding, they will now have the time to become a master coder. If you have a kid obsessed with starting a business, now they can.

It's also important I point out that we are not experts. We are parents who are trying to figure out the best journey for our family. I don't have a teaching degree and in fact was extremely against homeschooling for the first six years I had school-aged kids. The number-one greatest lesson I've learned through this process is that we have *choices* when it comes to our children's education. Learning isn't one size fits all. There are many alternative paths we can take.

Hopefully, *The 5-Hour School Week* inspires you to go after the very best version of your life, for yourself and your kids, and possibly create a 5-Hour School Week of your very own!

INTRODUCTION

OUR STORY

There are some things one can only achieve by a deliberate leap in the opposite direction.

—FRANZ KAFKA

It's 8:00 on a Monday morning, right in the middle of the school year. For the first time in years, my kids aren't stressed, and neither am I. We're not pounding out last-minute homework, scrambling for the carpool, or yelling to get into the bathroom.

In the kitchen, instead, I hear Madelyn teaching Charlotte how to make pancakes. The two younger kids, Isabel and Brax, sleep in their rooms blissfully. Here in the living room, I'm quietly planning a day of education that includes opening a bank account, shopping for groceries, and going on a hike.

Come 9:00 a.m., we will spend an hour on math, and I'll have time to squeeze in a fun reading activity, making sure we get in our five hours of academics this week. Maddie is teaching herself geometry, and Charlotte can't wait to start her times tables. Tomorrow, we'll probably skip math because Maddie wants to dedicate some serious time to her travel-binder business. The other two girls will be lost in a chess tournament against each other for a good portion of the day, which means I may actually get some laundry done.

Next week, we're heading to Chicago, and I'm working on that list as well. We'll visit the dinosaurs at the Field Museum, hit the aquarium, and dive into a world-famous deep-dish pizza.

Aaron pops in from his home office. "Hey, it turns out I have to be in Boston for a meeting right after Chicago. Let's make it a doubleheader."

"Awesome," I say. Then I start Googling the Tea Party Museum, Plymouth Village, and the Freedom Trail because I know we're *all* going to Boston. It's a city packed with history—a lesson around every corner. This is our new life!

OUR REMARKABLE JOURNEY

The opposite of bravery is not cowardice, but conformity.

—ROBERT ANTHONY

Our family has embarked on a remarkable journey. It's a journey filled with wonder, togetherness, and learning. You could call it homeschooling. Or unschooling. Or maybe world-schooling.

Aaron and I call it the 5-Hour School Week, and we think it's the ultimate education hack. Why? Because our kids aren't *just* finding out about the American Revolution by throwing tea into Boston Harbor, figuring out how to run a business by actually running a business, or learning how to stand on their own two feet by hiking. They're also making rapid progress in math and science, composition and spelling, history and foreign languages, and all those other important, book-based academics.

They're doing it all in about five hours of focused attention each week.

The 5-Hour School Week is not your mother's homeschooling. We all live in a new world of resources—thanks to the World Wide Web, all material is literally just a click away. There is no subject, topic, or problem that cannot be solved in your very own home. It's a world full of apps, programs, how-to videos, and curricula available to you, often at little to no cost. This new world is also filled with aquariums, planetariums, children's museums, nature discovery centers, educational exhibits, and national parks.

In this book, Aaron and I want to show you how you can use this new world to escape the traditional schooling trap—along with its endless classroom hours, unlimited stress, long nights of homework, and truly awful Monday mornings.

Once you've decided you want to escape, we'll show you how to reconnect with your schooled-out kids and redesign your lives together. You'll see how to teach all the real-world skills school has never been able to teach: how to plan a day, manage money, keep house, and talk to adults in the real world.

Here's what Aaron and I have discovered: *you can beat the system*. You can have relaxed, happy kids who look forward to learning. You can avoid hours of your kids sitting at a desk, boring textbooks, burnt-out teachers, fights over homework, and discontented mornings and nights.

Embrace the 5-Hour School Week and you can take your family on your own remarkable journey. I promise you will get a hundred times closer to your kids. You will make your family into a team, and you will rediscover the joys of parenthood. You will no longer feel like you are just surviving as a parent, because your family will begin to thrive like never before!

I also promise you will never again get up at midnight to fill in a reading slip for your six-year-old. Never again build a school project while your seven-year-old is sleeping. Never again watch your eight-year-old throw up from fear before a spelling test.

I've been there. I've done that. And I'm never going back.

I can't wait to tell you more about our lives today. But to explain how we got to the 5-Hour School Week, I have to take you back to the beginning of our journey, when our three oldest were in—you guessed it—*school*.

Here's how that life worked for my kids and their old mom, "discontented Kaleena," and how we discovered "happy Kaleena" through the 5-Hour School Week. I have a feeling you might just feel like I'm narrating your life!

THE WAY IT USED TO BE

The alarm fires off like a starting gun. It's 5:30 a.m. If I hit snooze, I get three precious minutes of planning before the race begins.

Lying in the dark, I go through my crisis list: *It's Izzy's turn for show-and-tell, but she forgot to prepare. Whatever she brings has to start with a V. What starts with V? No way can she bring a glass vase to school. Vaseline? Too weird. Maddie needs me to sign a permission slip for something. Did I lose it, or does she still have it in her backpack? Wait...Maddie needs that permission slip for a field trip to the city tomorrow. Right. I was "volunteered" to chaperone. Forty-five minutes to the city, two-hour play, forty-five minutes back. Tomorrow's shot. Remember that. Today, Maddie needs the money up front, in cash, with the permission slip, together in an envelope. I'm sure I can find an envelope.*

In the quiet rooms beyond, I'm aware of my four sweet children sleeping deeply: Madelyn, just eight; Charlotte, six; Isabel, five; and Brax, just six months. I picture their regular, gentle breathing. Their undisturbed dreams. Come 6:00 a.m., I'll have to rouse the three girls with the same shocking news I deliver at dawn five days a week: time to get ready for school. And none of them wishes it were true.

Six minutes to get the three groggy girls awake and moving toward the bathroom. That leaves twenty-four minutes to get three *still-groggy* girls showered and dressed, get bows in hair, and get the girls to the kitchen for breakfast. Then it's a race to eat, get the backpacks assembled, lunches packed, coats found, and get them into the minivan by 7:15...Wait! *OMG, as of bedtime last night, Charlotte still hadn't filled in her reading slip!*

If baby Brax wakes, all will be lost.

A QUESTION IN THE DARK

In the twenty seconds before the alarm sounds again, all I can think is, "How does this life make any sense at all?!" The girls haven't had enough sleep. They're going to fight me every step of the way. From the moment I wake them, it will be stress and conflict. Once again, school will get the best of my girls. Aaron and I will get the leftovers.

Aaron is still snoring, and it's not fair to wake him and ask this question. He has his own big day of work. Maybe he can pick up the girls later—maybe get in a little dad time before the crush of soccer, karate, times tables, reading slips, history homework, and all the rest of life and education we need to pack in before bed. Of course, after school is the girls' worst time—with the exception of mornings. By that time, the girls are so beat they don't want to talk to anyone, even their dad.

"How was your day?"

"Fine."

"Learn anything interesting?"

"No."

"Who'd you play with?"

"I don't know."

This is about the most I can squeeze out of them. Sadly, I realize I haven't had a quality conversation with any of my kids in weeks.

The alarm fires off again. No more time for philosophizing. Twenty-seven minutes to make coffee, throw together breakfasts, and assemble three custom lunch boxes. Heaven forbid I do something crazy like pack PB&J or have all three enjoy the same type of food.

Outside, a beautiful dawn rises, but in my kitchen, it brings only hurry and fear. The lunch boxes are lined up, and right at 6:00 a.m., I begin the wake-up drill. Teeth brushed? Hair washed? Correct school uniform? I turn on the shower, just to give them the idea.

"No, Mom, not *V*. It's *W* this week," says Izzy, as she shuffles into the kitchen. It takes me a second to remember that she's talking about show-and-tell. "They went right to *W*. I thought maybe watermelon. Can I take a watermelon to school?"

"No, Sweetie. I don't happen to have a watermelon." Before I can come up with a good idea, Brax starts crying. We have to leave in ten minutes or we'll be late. *W...W...* Window cleaner? Wax candle? Charlotte can only find one shoe. Maddie left her coat at school but is too cold to leave the house without it.

At 7:12, Aaron walks in to help with the final countdown, and I give him a desperate look. He finds Charlotte's shoe. He finds a stuffed walrus toy for the *W* assignment. There's no time to ask him the question that is always on my mind: Is this really all there is to this life? Is this really all parenting is?

A MINIVAN OF UNHAPPY KIDS

At 7:20 a.m., just five minutes behind schedule, I'm driving a minivan full of unhappy girls still knocking off the sleep. Brax sits uneasily in the car seat; my third cup of coffee sits in the cupholder. I have been rushed, rushed, rushed from the moment my feet hit the floor.

I should be proud to have made it to the minivan one more time. It's tough when all I hear is discontent. Maddie has a test, and it brings her usual anxiety. She's a star in the classroom, but that's not good enough for her—or her teacher, who expects more and more from a *star*. "I just can't get past my multiplication test! I won't be able to move on!" she cries out. I try to talk her down during the twenty-minute drive. I try to talk all of them down, but the conversation consists of nothing but anxiety. A key issue for conversation? Which friends are getting along. Which are not.

"I really hope Jane and Chelsea made up this weekend and they're not fighting at school *again*, because it really stresses me out," despairs Maddie. "I wonder who I'll get to play with today," worries Izzy. Then, more ominously, "I don't want to go to school. I don't feel good."

But of course, no matter what, *I still have to take them to school. It's what good parents do. It's what we did as kids. It's what we are "supposed" to do.*

RISING EXPECTATIONS

Both Aaron and I had public school teachers for parents, and we really believed in the idea of public education. However, we had found a Christian private school close by—not too eye-wateringly expensive—and it had sold us on its amazing academics. "Your kids will learn more, learn quicker, in a safer, faith-based environment!" they said.

Great school. Amazing teachers. Nice community. Unfortunately, they were right about incredible academics.

Even in preschool, the kids—and the parents—felt the pressure. Seriously, the show-and-tell by the letters thing was a big deal during preschool; the project that was originally supposed to be fun and creative turned competitive and stressful. On F day, I'd suggest a toy frog, but of course, another kid had already done "frog." On X day, yours could not be yet another kid bringing an X-ray. You had to be unique, an original. Parents would nervously scan the show-and-tell box to make sure their child had brought something no one else had thought of.

When Maddie started kindergarten, we had intended to send her to public school but were convinced she needed that full day, compared to the half day she'd get at a public school. We figured, of course kids should be in school for seven hours a day! Kindergarten's the most important year. They have to learn to read, right? I didn't want her to "fall behind" by the time she was six!

By the time she left kindergarten, Maddie was reading at a second-grade level. I was thrilled, but the school told me we'd want to be sure to keep up on that this summer or she'd fall behind in first grade. "Oh my gosh," I said to Aaron, "we need to put Maddie in summer school so she doesn't fall behind!" How could we argue with making her smarter and more successful? That first summer, we spent a ridiculous amount of time and money so that our soon-to-be first grader would be able to make the grade.

By the time Maddie was in first grade, she was reading at a fourth-grade level, but every day she was pushed to do more. It was never enough for her or for the school. Following right in her stressed-out footsteps were my two younger girls.

"HEY, WAIT A MINUTE!" MOMENTS

Our first "Hey, wait a minute!" moment came with something Maddie said one night after dinner.

She was seven years old, in second grade. It had been a long day: we'd done soccer. We'd completed the math homework. Now, thank heavens, even dinner had been accomplished. As always, I turned to my eldest daughter and said, "Okay, now you have to go and do your twenty minutes of reading so I can fill out your reading slip."

"I earned enough points to take the night off, my teacher said..." I heard myself say, "No, you can't take a night off!" I honestly felt panicked. *We can't take our foot off the gas pedal. We need to keep encouraging her to be great. If she's reading at a fifth-grade level, she could be reading at a sixth-grade level!* But Maddie was confused. "I'm one of the best students in my class! I'm reading bigger books than everyone else! I should be able to take one night off!" she cried.

Later, in bed, Aaron and I looked at each other, and for

the first time we spoke aloud *The Question*: "What kind of life is this?" Maybe our second grader had a point. Maybe she was right to ask, "When is enough, enough?" But there were no answers, just a lot of fear of falling behind and not being "good enough."

Still, we let the madness continue.

In the beginning of her kindergarten year, at the age of five, Isabel could only read thirty words. It was a crisis! Her teacher gave me a worried look: "You know, we've really got to work on this. I'm concerned."

That conversation about Izzy put me right back in "Hey, wait a minute!" mode. I looked at her teacher and thought, *Just why, exactly, are we concerned? What difference does it make?*

It was one of many moments that continued to guide us toward pulling our kids completely out of school.

ADULTS ACE A THIRD-GRADE ASSIGNMENT

The next big "Hey, wait a minute!" moment came in the third grade, when Maddie was given a difficult—one might say *high-stakes*—assignment.

Everyone in her class was required to build a complete

board game based on a book they'd been reading. It seemed a bit pointless, and I muttered to Aaron, "I don't think she's learning anything from these projects, and one of us usually ends up doing more than half the work."

We talked it over, and ultimately, we decided Maddie was going to do this thing. She was going to learn plenty from organizing the project *all by herself*. I went to Maddie and encouraged her: "You're old enough to carry this through, sweetheart. I know you're capable."

I was impressed when she expressed a clear vision for her game. The book told the story of a child's spiritual journey, so Maddie planned to build a Candy Land-type game board, where players progressed from one important life moment to the next. She created a list of everything she needed, and I took her to buy the materials. I taught her to use a glue gun, but I was careful not to help her flesh out the vision or physically help her build the project so she'd truly learn from the experience.

It took my third grader a whole week—but that game board was 100 percent her vision and her work. As for me, I couldn't have been prouder. I was looking forward to the upcoming open house, when all the game boards would be displayed.

Maybe you already guessed the end of this story...

At the open house, Maddie's was one of the lowest-quality efforts on display. In fact, most of the boards were unbelievably impressive. They lit up with dazzling LEDs. They played music when you pushed buttons. They were executed with adult, even professional, detail—because, of course, *adults had constructed them.* When I told one girl she had a cool board, she replied with a shrug, "Yeah, my dad stayed up all night and did it for me." Maddie was deeply disappointed, even embarrassed. She said, "Mom, mine doesn't even light up!"

When we got home from that open house, Aaron and I had a major "Hey, wait a minute!" moment. In bed, we stared into the darkness and began to ask, now more seriously, "What are we doing? How did this assignment, one that was supposed to be fun and creative, manage to destroy the very joy of being independent and capable?" We didn't have an answer.

THE CRISIS DEEPENS

After that, nearly every night, we'd turn to each other and sigh. It had happened again. We were all so deep into the rat race that we hadn't gotten to spend any meaningful time together. None at all.

I'd tell Aaron what I'd once only thought to myself: "I got the worst of my kids again today. I am giving to someone else the very best of them, and I am constantly just being handed the leftovers. I never even held Izzy today. I never even looked into her face. My entire job as a mother now seems to be, 'Keep your kids supplied with food and push them to keep going through the process.' Basically, I'm just a drill sergeant working for the school."

Aaron would do the math: a seven-hour school day really meant a nine- or ten-hour school day, when you count the driving and the homework. During the week, the only time we got to be "parents"—as in actively talking to our girls—was at dinner, but even dinner was rushed. They had to do those endless reading assignments and still hit bed by nine.

I thought being a mom was going to be *a lot better* than this. Like, I thought I was going to make an impact. I had big dreams for my children, and yet someone else had them the majority of the time. That in itself gave me very little room to say how they spent their time and what they were learning. Sometimes tears came to my eyes. "Oh my God, Maddie is nine. That means half of her childhood is already over. I don't even know who she is. I don't even know what she's passionate about." I was sad and couldn't see a solution in sight.

I thought it would help if I got more involved in the school. So I began volunteering for more and more events. I even became PTA president. Yet my girls seemed to be getting less and less happy each morning, and crankier and crankier at the end of each day. And honestly, so was I!

Come fourth grade, Maddie was reading at an eighth-grade level. Only now, it started to alarm me. *Hey, wait a minute. This might not be so great. My fourth grader is now reading material she shouldn't really be exposed to at the age of nine. Maybe we should slow it down*, I started to think. But the playground chatter almost always centered on "accomplishments," and it had become important to have kids in the top reading groups, with the highest grades, and winning the spelling bees. I would hear the moms of older kids talk about a 4.0 just not being "good enough." If I wanted our kids to attend a good college, then a 4.5 with a ton of AP classes would have to be the goal!

It dawned on me: there will be no reprieve from this. We were literally setting our kids up for a lifetime of jumping through meaningless hoops. And to top it off, we would have zero time to create a lasting impact or memories with our children because fifty-plus hours a week, they would be sitting at a desk.

HOW COULD WE LIVE BIG?

In spite of all our angst and each conversation leading to how this life made us unhappy, there was nothing we felt we could do about it. This was just what we had to do for our kids to be successful—send them to school and push them harder.

What finally got us heading in a new direction was not thinking about "education" at all. It was thinking about how to live a better life—as in living "a big life." Aaron is a real estate entrepreneur, and he began meeting with a mastermind group of other entrepreneurs. Together, they read motivational literature, help each other accomplish goals, and brainstorm. One of Aaron's favorites is *The 4-Hour Workweek* by Timothy Ferriss. Aaron got excited about Ferriss and his "live life big" motto. Over time, Aaron even began coaching and speaking on stage about life hacks based on the 4-Hour principles.

For us, living big meant travel. We were dying to take our kids to visit national parks and see the world, but we had always assumed that traveling with four young children would be too difficult. Hustling kids onto planes might be tough—but the biggest problem? Once again, school. We'd look at dates and places, and we'd decide they had to be in school. If we pulled them out for a couple of weeks, they'd miss something incredibly crucial. They'd fall behind and never be able to make it up, and we'd cause some kind of disaster for them.

We had the resources, and Aaron often had to travel a

lot for work anyway, but as a family we were limited to Christmas break, spring break, summer, or the occasional three-day holiday weekend—all of which are the absolute worst times to travel.

Summer presented the greatest irony. You'd think we'd find serious travel possibilities in summer. But like everyone else, we were encouraged to keep our kids in summer school or camp most of the season—three or four camps sometimes.

When we did try to travel with the whole gang during one of our crowded little vacation windows, we were always too rushed, everything was booked, the other travelers were cranky, our kids were too stressed, and they didn't yet know how to sit still on airplanes. When we didn't have a good time, people would say, "I told you not to try to travel with four young kids!" But I knew there were people who did it, and I wanted to be one of those people!

THE VICE PRINCIPAL SPILLS THE BEANS ON "SCHOOL"

Two events helped push us over the line. The first was a confession from Matt Beaudreau, then vice principal of our kids' private school. The second was a trip to Yosemite.

Matt had been at the school about three years. I loved

Matt. He was great with the kids. He knew how to talk on their level and bring out their best, and he just seemed to have a fresh perspective on everything. When I heard he was leaving to start his own school, I was bummed, and I invited him out for coffee.

Matt began by telling me about the school he was starting. It would be an "Acton Academy," part of a chain of entrepreneurial-based schools, running from kindergarten through high school. He described Acton's cool alternative educational model, where independent kids learned things that mattered to them—and often walked out of school already owning their own businesses. The kids picked their own topics to learn, and the school encouraged travel. Learning was experience-based: instead of teaching math, they'd get the kids interested in building a rocket; then the kids would teach themselves math to do it right. Even reading and writing came *as a result of doing.*

I drank up every word—not only because I knew he was passionate about education and kids, but because, for the first time, everything I heard actually made sense.

Then Matt, a man I deeply respected, who was vice principal of the school my kids attended, the school where I was then PTA president, said this: "I could never send my own kids to a school like this. The days are far too long, and kids this age should not have homework. They should be able to explore things that they're really passionate about. Before my kids get old enough to go to school, I have to open a school where I would feel comfortable sending them."

I stared, openmouthed.

Matt had suggested I read *Free-Range Kids* by Lenore Skenazy, and *Free to Learn* by Peter Gray. I immediately ordered these books from Amazon, but they sat on my nightstand, unread, collecting dust. We didn't yank the girls out of school or make any educational changes at all. However, the conversation changed dramatically. Where there had been a lot of fear, now there was a new excitement. It occurred to us, *In theory, we could do something completely different than what we are doing.*

But something else still had to happen; we needed one more shove in the right direction. And then we went to Yosemite.

YOSEMITE STEPS IN

A whole year earlier, after a nudge from one of our friends, we'd found a half-off deal for a ten-day trip to Yosemite National Park. We had spent some time camping there together prior to kids and had absolutely loved it, but the kids had never been. The trip was scheduled for May, during the school year, but it was so cheap that we booked it without being sure we'd have the courage to pull the girls out when the time came.

Now the date was fast approaching, and Matt had given us that last ounce of courage.

Aaron and I said to ourselves, "We'll make the trip educational, and the kids will bring along their homework so they don't fall behind." Believe me, plenty of drama came with pulling the girls out of school for ten days. We had to make no end of reassurances and arrangements with their teachers, but once we passed through the park gates, we knew it was worth it. After we'd checked in, and while unpacking our bags in the little dorm-like room, it occurred to us that we'd accidentally left all the schoolwork behind!

It wasn't intentional; it just happened. With spotty cell service and no internet, Aaron wasn't going to be able to get much work done either.

What was left? Yosemite. We didn't yet know we'd started our new life, but we had. For an entire ten days we lived as a family and immersed ourselves in time with our kids. In nature. Without technology.

For starters, we challenged ourselves physically. We took

four- or five-hour hikes with our little kids—hikes where we'd see no other little kids. We'd say to the gang, "In order to see cool stuff, we have to go through the effort, and it will be hard." We learned a lot about our kids' personalities as they wrestled with dangerous wet steps and steep climbs. They learned a lot about themselves as they faced some big fears as well.

We also discovered all the amazing resources the park had organized, seemingly just for us. We did an open-air tour where the ranger taught us about the geology and wildlife of Yosemite. Every night, the park held informational ranger talks around a campfire or theater setting.

WHAT KIDS ARE ACTUALLY SUPPOSED TO DO

The kids were wowed and amazed by everything. They learned and learned with no effort and pure joy. All day we'd talk with the girls and just *be* their teachers, on whatever subject arose. Nature also became their teachers... and so did the rangers...and the whole earth. During one of our conversations, I remember Charlotte saying, "Wow, we didn't know that you knew all this stuff!" She wasn't kidding. In fact, at that point, I don't think the girls even realized Aaron and I had an education, that we were in any way qualified to be their teachers and their guides on this earth.

Before that trip to Yosemite, I would have said, "No, my kids absolutely could not do a hike like Nevada Falls. It's too dangerous." But in those magical ten days, I saw how capable kids can be—anyone's kids. How resilient. I saw how good it was for them to find their own strength.

Suddenly, it hit me: *Wait a minute. This is what kids are supposed to do. It's what they have to do to become strong, balanced adults.* By the end of the week, even Maddie was less high-strung. It took a few days of nature, no internet, no TV, and no homework—but over those ten days, we began to see the cheerful kid we always knew was in there, the one who used to peek out only now and then.

On the drive home, Aaron and I looked at each other and said without words, *Hey, it's not too late, right?*

AN AMAZING TWO HOURS

We got home from Yosemite on a Sunday morning. After unpacking, we faced the harsh reality that all three girls had missed a week and a half of school—and we had forgotten to bring along their work. They'd not only missed the school-day lessons we were supposed to do with them, but *they were a week and a half behind on homework, too.*

As soon as we walked in the door, the magic of the trip

faded, and Maddie started to freak out: "Oh my God, I didn't do any homework at all. I'll never, ever catch up." The clock read noon, but we could all see it ticking its way again toward 5:30 Monday morning.

Aaron, in his calm way, said, "Let's just sit down, and we'll start trying to knock out as much as we can before bedtime." Later, he told me he was remembering his moonlighting as a 4-Hour Workweek coach. Plenty of times he had told others, "If you use extreme focus, you can get eight hours of work done in one hour. With no distractions, you can just do it."

I started cooking away in the kitchen while Aaron sat at the table with Madelyn and Charlotte. And guess what? *Two hours later, all their work was done.* No joke, in two hours, a week and a half of homework was finished.

Just as importantly, those two hours passed like no other homework session I could remember. No arguing. No fuss. No fighting. Just sitting and working with their dad and having, yes, *fun*.

MAKING SHORT WORK OF LONG DIVISION

The big issue was long division. Maddie's teacher had intended to introduce this important subject to her class while Maddie was gone, and Maddie had never seen it before. Lo and behold, Aaron taught it to her in about an hour, right there at the table.

Aaron said that session had worked so well because the girls were super focused and motivated. They were able to go exactly as fast as they *could* go, and the instant they had a question, he was there to answer it. The girls could focus and keep moving forward *without a pause*. In a normal classroom, that's not how it works. Kids don't get their questions answered right away, and the teacher teaches at one level to everyone. He said, "When I taught Maddie long division, I could break it down in pieces exactly *for her*. I could see what she was grasping and what she was not. Within an hour, she was working long division problems like a champ."

When the work was done, our whole family experienced a genuine epiphany—a moment of amazement and realization. *Wow, we had ten days where we learned so much about life and nature—and so much about each other. We didn't miss a thing at school, because we got all that homework done in a couple of hours. We did it all. We lived at a level we didn't know was even possible.*

The next day, all the Amuchasteguis woke up with new confidence in ourselves as a family.

AHEAD OF THE CLASS

When Aaron picked Maddie up from school that Monday afternoon, she was totally excited. She said, "Dad, you won't believe it. I'm the *only* one in the class who knows long division. They didn't even get to it last week during class." In fact, Maddie was ahead of the whole class in pretty much everything. She'd done all the work intended for ten days in two hours and turned in worksheets and assignments that most of the class hadn't even started.

When Aaron brought Maddie home, we again looked at each other for a few minutes without even talking.

I should mention that Maddie's class worked on long division for three more tedious weeks. Night after night, she'd bring home the worksheets and, of course—because we are rule followers and had decided that if we would be staying in school, we would be respectful of school assignments—we allowed precious family time to be interrupted by material she had already mastered.

Now every school topic seemed like long division, drawn out endlessly and unnecessarily by an outdated system.

DELIBERATE WORLD-SCHOOLING BEGINS

Just a month after our Yosemite revelation, we made our first deliberate world-schooling trip. Aaron had a convention to attend in Miami, after which he planned to join his entrepreneurial group for a gathering in Philadelphia. He said, "Let's pull the kids out of school. Let them play on the beach in Miami and then see the Liberty Bell in Philly. It will be cool."

By now, I was all in. I'd seen how much we could learn on a trip, and how absurdly easy it was to keep up with schoolwork. On the spot, I decided we would just make Aaron's idea work: *Hey, Charlotte is learning about George Washington; let's take her to his house in Philadelphia and to Liberty Hall. Maddie's learning about the Constitution; let's show her the real thing, along with the place where the first American flag was sewn.*

Thanks to Google, it was easy to figure out that Miami had a children's museum, a zoo, an aquarium, and interesting parks—I mean, just for starters. In no time, I'd built out an itinerary of everything I could do while Aaron was working.

Sure, I was nervous. I'd never been to Miami, and there I'd be, driving around four kids by myself. In this new world, however, not only can you Google children's museums, but you can navigate by GPS. The children's museum was amazing. The science museum was amazing, and the kids didn't want to leave, even after five hours. On a weekday, we were practically the only ones there. All these magnificent, multimillion-dollar facilities, designed by smart people and staffed by brilliant docents, were just waiting for us to arrive.

In Fort Lauderdale, we took a boat tour to see how homes were built on the canal. We watched someone wrestle a crocodile. We took big airboats through the Everglades.

Did the kids learn more in four days of experiencing Miami than they would have learned in four days of going to school? You bet. Just as importantly, I learned I could world-school by myself for a full day with four kids. Driving along in the rented minivan, I thought, *Hey, I'm capable of doing this anywhere, finding great resources and handling the kids, even if Aaron is away. I can find education every single place that we go. I can turn every single situation into a learning experience—every life moment.*

Some of that learning would replace book learning, but much of it would teach real-life skills that books cannot: such as standing patiently in lines, using public transportation, being flexible, and acting like a member of society. It was exciting to think I could teach my kids many things I did not learn until I was in my twenties.

In Miami, everything I saw became a lesson, and I began to see the world as our classroom: not just places we had to fly to but also places within driving distance back home.

We could learn anywhere if we were focused and deliberate in our intentions. In the evenings, Aaron joined us for family time without homework: just us talking and learning together as we did back in the cabin at Yosemite.

Oh, and yeah, the schoolwork got done, too—quickly and efficiently. No big deal. The plan was working, and as we flew to Philadelphia, my mind was on fire. I said to Aaron, "You know what? We're totally done living in the box."

"SCHOOL TEACHES THE WRONG STUFF"

In Philadelphia, we took the kids to the President's House, where George Washington lived during the early part of the American Revolution. They stood where the Declaration of Independence was signed. An unexpected lesson, but perhaps most important, we heard Jim Sheils speak at a family conference we were attending. Sheils wrote a book called *The Family Board Meeting*, and like Matt Beaudreau, he blew our minds.

At the core of Sheils's book lies a once-per-quarter, one-on-one meeting with each of your kids. You turn off the TV and the phones for four or five hours and talk—have a real conversation. His "education matrix" struck us even more deeply.

To introduce the matrix, Sheils asked, in essence, what

the most important challenges were that the audience had faced in life. In reply, people shared all kinds of life's highs and lows: money challenges, work challenges, health challenges, family challenges. And then he asked this dangerous question: "Each of those challenges required skills in order to be met. Of those skills, how many did you learn in school?"

The reply from every single person in the room? "None."

Nothing anyone in the room had learned in school had helped them with life's biggest challenges. His conclusion? School should teach you what you need to learn in life. Instead, it teaches you information you can't often use.

Sheils then laid out what he called his matrix of things people *should* learn to make their lives succeed. His matrix included making decisions based on healthy risk-taking, learning the time value of money, learning how to invest, understanding options on paying bills, learning how to maintain good credit. The tilt was entrepreneurial, but all his items struck a chord. Life requires hard lessons that we must teach to our children. Even the most academically educated among us, the people with multiple degrees from major colleges, learn *none* of these lessons in their expensive classrooms. None.

When the room fell silent, Sheils asked, "Why do we outsource education when our most important resource is our children? Why would we let someone else teach our kids what *they* think our kids are supposed to learn, rather than what *we* think our kids are supposed to learn? Why would we do that?"

PRACTICING WHAT AARON PREACHED

A few months after Philadelphia, Aaron was on stage at a self-help conference talking about how people could adapt Tim Ferriss's 4-Hour Workweek principles to their own lives. He had an audience of about 150 people. "The presentation was going really well, and I had a lot of great interactions with the audience. My basic message? 'Hey, everyone in this room works too much. You should go out and live more and make your lives better. Fill your life with hobbies instead of work. Just put in a highly focused hour or two a day, without distractions, and then pursue your passions and your family life.'"

Aaron said that right at the end of the Q&A, a woman stood up and asked, "If you advocate this for everyone here, and if you're telling us we should be working only four hours a week, how do you apply that to your kids' education?" He was stunned. Obviously, we felt it was time for a change, but put like that, it brought our entire problem into focus, and the solution became so clear. He thought, *Wow, I'm telling all these people to radically change their lives, but my kids are still going to school forty hours a week.*

A couple of days later, Aaron called me from his business trip. He'd bought the 5hourschoolweek.com URL and had already applied for a trademark. Other ideas from the Ferriss book began linking together in our heads. Ferriss talks about how, if you do things right in the new world, you can work from anywhere. If you pack light, you can travel and live in exciting, exotic places while still earning a living remotely.

Well, why couldn't all those same techniques work for education, too?

THE LAST DAY OF SCHOOL—EVER

Aaron was confident in my ability to homeschool, but he also knew homeschooling would fall mostly on me. He came to me and said, "I'll support you in whatever you want to do. Just please, please make a decision." I was less confident that I could pull this off and really struggled with pulling the trigger. "What if I really get this wrong? Education is so important. What if this in fact hinders the girls rather than helps them?" I was stressed—really, really stressed.

Meanwhile, he was planning our next big trip. He'd heard

that the volcano on the Big Island of Hawaii was erupting, and he said, "Can you imagine the educational value of seeing a volcano up close?" Right away, he booked us for three weeks in Hawaii during Thanksgiving, to heck with school. "And actually," he mentioned, "I have a conference in Arizona the second week in November, so let's start the trip all together in Arizona. It's pretty interesting there, too."

I just nodded as I wrote out the checks for the start of the school year—never mind that the kids would be gone nearly all of November. Despite all our revelations, school still had its hold on us, and come September, classes kicked back into gear, 5:30 a.m. alarm and all.

"I THINK THIS IS IT"

Then, finally, I did it.

On November 1, the school was closed for parent-teacher conferences. Aaron was out of town on a business trip, and as I drove to the conferences, somehow it all came together. Without thinking, I called him from my cell and said, "I think this is it. I'm taking them out of school. I'm gonna do it."

As usual, Aaron just replied, "I'll support you in whatever you decide."

After I hung up, I said a little prayer: "If You know any reason why school is still important for us, please let me know right now. If You don't, *this is it*. I'm showing up, and I'm literally telling the teachers, 'I'm pulling my kids out.'"

Madelyn's fourth-grade teacher greeted me with a big smile and started in about my amazing daughter. She told me how Madelyn received excellent grades, got along with everyone, and loved being the teacher's pet. Then, as a fatal blow, she added, "But let's try to get her moving a little faster. Let's try to increase her reading. Let's get her more confident in her math skills by doing more homework at night."

The switch flipped in my head, and I heard myself saying, "None of that's going to be necessary, because Maddie's no longer going to be enrolled in school." Somehow, I restrained myself from adding, *Are you crazy? You just got through telling me she's an exceptional student, and now you say you still want more?* Instead, I was very nice. I was very calm. I said, "You're a great teacher, and I love what you do here. Thank you so much for your time and your commitment. I'll let the principal know, so you don't have to worry about that. I'll come back with Maddie next week to gather up her belongings."

I'd gone in with butterflies, but I left on cloud nine. The other two conferences went similarly. Surprisingly to me, not a single person at the school disagreed with our decision or reasoning. In fact, one of the other teachers, whom we deeply loved, wistfully agreed and told me they wished they could do the same for their child. I went skipping back to my car, where I called Aaron to say, "Here we go, Honey, starting right now. I did it."

When I walked into the house, I repeated, "Okay, I did it," and the girls knew exactly what I meant. They cheered and yelled out, "Good job, Mom! We're so proud of you." That was a funny thing to say, but of course, we'd talked about homeschooling endlessly, and they weren't sure I was capable of making the move.

I told them I didn't have this all figured out yet, but we'd buy some cool supplies and get all set up and comfortable and then work it out together as we went.

When I told my girls they would get to learn the topics they wanted to learn, they cheered again. I finished with, "Tomorrow, you'll wake up when you want to wake up. You'll wake up rested. You're going to get yourselves in the shower and get yourselves ready for the day. I'm not going to do that anymore. You're going to be responsible for yourselves from now on."

Charlotte, our middle daughter, did say, "Well, what about our friends?" I was ready: "We're still going to be in soccer. We're still going to go to the same gym. We're going to make time and space for you to see your friends as much as possible, and we hope to make new friends on our new journey."

"My friends aren't going to be homeschooled, too," she observed.

"That's right. They'll be in school during the day while we're doing our own activities."

"I don't have to wake up at 6:00 a.m. tomorrow?" asked Izzy.

"No," I repeated. "I want you to be rested."

And Izzy smiled.

OUR NEW LIFE

Mornings used to be my most hated time of day. Now they're my favorite. Dawn no longer brings fear. It brings a promise of the joyful and the unexpected—because mornings are the time my kids come to me and say, "What are we going to learn today?" or even better, "Here's what we want to learn today."

That very first morning of our new lives was unforgettable.

The girls weren't up at 6:00, but they were up at 7:00—well before me. By the time I walked into the kitchen, all three were wearing chef's hats and aprons, cooking up scrambled eggs. I just sat and watched, with tears in my eyes.

By the end of day two, Aaron and I walked into the kitchen and found a full restaurant, with a sales poster and a menu. The girls had organized themselves into chef, server, and maître d'. An account book showed how the profits would be divided.

A few mornings later, Charlotte woke up to say, "I want to learn about cheetahs, 'cause they're my favorite animal." So we all began to learn about cheetahs. Maddie decided she was going to teach Charlotte how to write a report about cheetahs, and for the rest of the day, they were Googling facts and diving into *National Geographic Kids*.

Miraculously, my fourth grader was teaching my first grader about rough drafts, credible resources, and paragraph structure. *Both girls were having a great time.* At the end of the day, Charlotte told me, "Mom, listen to everything I learned about cheetahs today."

Reading. Writing. Geography. Zoology. Biology. Just like that.

Plenty of mornings, we're piling into a car or an airplane and heading out on another world-schooling adventure. As you have figured out by now, our new life includes plenty of travel: around town, around the country, and—more and more—around the world. We've spent serious time in amazing cities and jaw-dropping national parks of our own great country. After our honeymoon, we hadn't had the opportunity to leave the country. In our new life, we've started exploring this great globe, starting in Canada, then on to Cuba, England, Sri Lanka, South Africa, Zimbabwe, Zambia, and Haiti. Our experiences have felt surreal, and I'm excited to see where we go next!

We used to travel to lie on beaches, but now we travel to experience life and immerse ourselves in history, culture, and practical experiences. We find traveling educational collections such as the recent *Bodies* and *Titanic* exhibits in Vegas and spelunking caves in Oregon and Texas.

Everything excites the girls. Everything interests them. Everything sparks questions and more questions. We have rediscovered our children, and they have rediscovered us: our girls will now discuss anything and everything with their parents. Aaron and I know their passions and their fears, their hopes, their dreams, and their growing pains.

Oh, and we get our academics done—in those five hours a week.

TRAVEL OR NO TRAVEL

Remember, travel is our added thing for our family, but it's not the way everyone will choose to implement this homeschool technique. Our journey started out simply, just exploring local museums and parks, and now we've been able to do more extensive travels.

In this book, we've brought together stories from other families who have adopted the 5-Hour School Week and adapted it to fit their needs and passions. You may find helpful tips and ideas you can try with your kids and then develop your own unique learning plan to help your kids love learning.

This schooling method is for *anybody*!

CONFIDENCE

If I had to name the one greatest benefit my kids have received from the 5-Hour School Week to date, I'd have to say *confidence*.

Later, I'll tell you how my nine-year-old recently had the confidence to stand up at a conference of entrepreneurs and talk through her online business ideas. For now, let me just say that our girls have more confidence in themselves than they ever had when they were in school. They're confident in their friendships, confident talking to adults, confident handling themselves in new situations, and confident that they can learn whatever they need or want to learn.

Confidence brings a wonderful lack of stress. Where once I had anxiety-stricken, exhausted children, I now experience the simple joy of watching my kids be kids: happy, healthy kids who are passionate about learning.

Before we began this journey, I would wake up asking, "Does this life make any sense?" Now I wake up, pinch myself, and ask, "Is this really our life now? This is so cool."

HOW THE REST OF THIS BOOK WORKS

We've given you a taste of our personal journey. In the rest of this book, Aaron and I want to help you figure out how to start your own journey and build your own kids' confidence. That means dispelling some of the myths about homeschooling, but mostly it means establishing a model more appropriate to the new age we all inhabit.

We'll start by outlining the issues with conventional education, and we'll break down the myth that hours of homework and tedious blackboard time are the most efficient ways to educate a child.

Then we'll dig into the how-to of the 5-Hour School

Week and get you well beyond the limited education that schools provide—showing you how to teach your kids to love learning every single day. We'll show you that your family need not be alone in this journey, because the new world includes hundreds of homeschooling groups and social circles. We'll explain how you can practice the 5-Hour School Week on any budget, with the resources you have right at hand.

We'll show you how we're educating our girls about business, negotiation, and making real money in the real world. We'll even reproduce some of the ledgers from their own pretty impressive entrepreneurial efforts. (Hint: no lemonade stands.) We'll show how we get the girls excited about physical education and community service. A whole chapter will be devoted to debunking the myth that homeschooled kids are awkward or unsocial.

Most importantly, we want to crush the notion that you have no options, that you have to do it the way the system has always done it.

Why? Because you live in a new world of educational opportunity, and it's yours to hack.

THE PROBLEM WITH MAINSTREAM EDUCATION

What's wrong with school? Why does it always seem so staggeringly inefficient? Such a stunning waste of time and resources? No matter how good the teachers, how dedicated the staff, or how well-constructed the curriculum, mainstream education just *can't* work well in this day and age. Even for the academic subjects it's designed to teach, traditional school will always fall short.

When looking at our current education system, it's crucial to understand why and how school actually came to be. We have to imagine a much different time in history. Prior to organized, in-class school, children spent their days in the field or working in factories with their parents. With the enactment of child labor laws in the early 1900s, classrooms became the most popular place for children to spend their time, and the curriculum was formulated to produce top-notch factory workers. School was built on a "cookie-cutter" foundation because the government literally wanted to produce robot-type workers for the industrial age.

Times have changed. Factory jobs are few, and jobs requiring innovation and adaptability are the jobs of today. Our world has evolved, but schools are still stuck in the old system meant for a society long behind us. The changes they have made have added to the problems of our stunted education system rather than helped bring more innovation and creativity.

Let's start with class size. Most public schools are allowed to have up to thirty-two kids in a classroom, with one full-time teacher and one part-time aide. Aside from the chaos this crowd naturally produces, teachers are forced to teach to the slowest student in the class. That means any kid who is faster, any kid who has already learned the material—or any kid with a different learning style—will be held back. Teachers would love to give individualized attention, but they just have no opportunity. It's simply impossible.

When Aaron taught Maddie long division in a couple of

hours, he could do it because he was teaching her one-on-one. He could see exactly what she understood and what she did not, and he could respond to her questions immediately. *That meant Maddie was saved from wasting literally tens of hours in the classroom on this one subject.*

No doubt teachers would love to teach at the speed of the fastest students, but of course, that would leave most of the students in a lurch. Each day, the slower kids would fall further and further behind, spend extra hours on homework, or have to go to summer school.

The result? Up until the most advanced levels of high school, literally every student must move at the speed of the slowest kids and must adapt to a single teaching style. Children also have different strengths, so a child who may be at the head of the class in math might be slower to learn in English. As a result, at some points they are waiting on others, while at other times they are holding up the class. Even in a smaller class of ten or fifteen students, this problem leads to misery and boredom. No wonder kids tune out. No wonder they feel their time is wasted. No wonder classrooms have discipline problems.

In other words, even at a theoretical level, the system has been badly designed. Even the best teachers (and plenty aren't that great) have been set up to fail. Whether your kid is the best in the class or whether they're the slowest, they're not being served well.

In *The 4-Hour Workweek*, Tim Ferriss posits that the most efficient work occurs when a single person focuses on a problem, all by themselves. More people in an office? That leads to more distractions. More confusion. Less efficiency.

This same idea applies to learning. Fewer people *always* works better. The most efficient teaching methods involve one teacher and one student—after that, inefficiencies quickly occur. In fact, if you can pull it off, self-teaching works best of all.

THE TROUBLE WITH HOMEWORK

In the United States, the average kid spends fifty hours a week between commuting to school, sitting in a classroom, and doing homework after school.

That's simply insane. While there are jobs out there that require this kind of time-intensive labor, and even those that don't pay overtime for your dedication, this pace is setting them up for an unhealthy work environment. They will enter adulthood thinking these excessive expectations are normal and acceptable. Never, in any of our jobs, have Aaron or I ever worked a full day in an office, then come home and worked an additional one to three hours every single night without overtime pay (although entrepreneurship is a different story). Hopefully, neither have you.

> On average, kids are doing more than three hours of homework each night by the time they reach high school. This is on top of the full day of assignments, tests, and lectures they are required to have in class.[1]

This pace is setting them up for an unhealthy work environment and puts them in line for excessive and unhealthy choices and expectations. Don't we all want better for our kids?

How have we come to put that expectation on a seven-year-old? How dare we say to a young child, "You just spent eight or more hours commuting to school and sitting in a classroom—but guess what? It wasn't enough to learn the material. You now need to spend two more hours working at home."

As a school mother, this expectation made me downright angry. Every night, when my girls hauled out backpacks stuffed with homework, I felt so defeated. I kept thinking

---

1   Kelly Wallace, "Kids Have Three Times Too Much Homework, Study Finds; What's the Cost?" *CNN*, August 12, 2015, https://www.cnn.com/2015/08/12/health/homework-elementary-school-study/index.html.

to myself, *You had them for nearly eight hours; how is that not enough? When do I get them to myself? When do we get to enjoy each other?*

No doubt the increasingly huge volume of homework follows from the basic problem of classroom learning. When you have lots of kids in a class, the interruptions are constant, and even slow-paced learning fails. Every few minutes, someone raises their hand to ask a question or use the restroom, or a kid makes a joke. Then there's lunch and recess and paperwork and the crazy challenge of hitting seven subjects a day.

I've volunteered in many classrooms, and I know a school day means start and stop, start and stop. The teachers get distracted and sidetracked, then everyone loses ten minutes every time the teacher says, "Okay, kids, put away your math books. We're on to social studies."

In this environment, homework becomes the *only* way to learn anything. Why does homework...work? Because kids sit down without distractions for a focused period of time and learn. They move at their own pace, get personally involved with the material, and don't have to deal with all the inefficiencies of a lecture. *Homework works because it's the way people have always learned best.*

What's the obvious solution? Eliminate the classroom

and make the best possible use of this focused, individual time.

In this book, we call that focused solution the 5-Hour School Week.

GIVING PARENTS THE WORST OF THEIR KIDS

Little people are not meant to sit at desks for hours. Physically and mentally, they're just not able to do that—and of course, even adults find this kind of life intolerable. No one wants to line up in straight lines as someone blows a whistle, raise their hand every time they want to speak, or get a permission slip to use the toilet.

After seven or more hours packed into the "school box," some kids naturally blow up. All day they've been holding it together, and now they need to release the tension where they will not be punished: In the carpool. On their siblings. On their parents. If you watch, you can just see these kids combust.

Small children may simply fall apart from exhaustion. Their minds can't process everything that was pressed upon them or that occurred out on the playground. So, when they get home, they just shut down. That is, if they *do* go home. Usually, kids have more to do after school: soccer, piano, karate—or all three. Maybe, just maybe, right after their extracurriculars they can combust or shut down.

DO THE MATH

7 hours of school

1 hour of commuting time

2 to 3 hours of homework

7 days each week = 50 to 55 hours per week, our kids scramble to keep up with the rat race

Bottom line? School parents usually experience the very worst of their own children. They get the dregs. They cannot even properly function as parents because they cannot talk to their children when they are in these reduced states.

Mornings are cranky times. Mealtimes are rushed times. Family time—genuine time together creating memories and enjoying one another—is nearly nonexistent, and our dream of travel must be squeezed into brief weekend hours or stolen from programmed activities and homework.

Worse, parents often find themselves enforcers for the school's own rules and deadlines. In the introduction, I said I felt I was becoming a drill sergeant, working for my girls' private school. This, too, deeply interferes with the parent-child relationship.

Given the odds stacked against kids, it's no wonder that so many develop serious problems later on in life. Drug and alcohol dependencies, depression, and suicide rates are continually on the rise.[2] Why? Kids burn out before they finish high school. In fact, the successful kids often burn out first. Like Maddie, they are pushed and pushed by teachers and parents alike. High school high-achievers now often use uppers so they can concentrate longer and get a better GPA—often completing half of their first year of college before they have even graduated from high school.

Kids simply cannot cope with the life that society has created for them. They're cracking, exhausted, under the pressure of the system. They're addicted, depressed, discouraged, and lacking confidence, none of which I wanted for my kids.

Other children are becoming completely bored by the repetitive class curricula and endless hours in the box.

---

2   Kelly Posner, "Preventing Suicide: Teen Deaths Are on the Rise, but We Know How to Fight Back," *USA Today*, February 7, 2018, https://www.usatoday.com/story/opinion/2018/02/07/preventing-suicide-teen-deaths-rise-but-we-know-how-fight-back-kelly-posner-column/305206002/; Robert Preidt, "U.S. Teen Suicide Rates Continue to Rise," *MedicineNet.com*, August 29, 2018 in *JAMA Psychiatry*, https://www.medicinenet.com/script/main/art.asp?articlekey=205869.

I have a hard time believing that kids want and need to learn the history of the Civil War in the fifth grade. Then again in sixth grade. Then again in eighth. Then again in tenth. Then again...well, no doubt you remember the boredom, even if you don't remember Gettysburg.

THE ARTIFICIAL SOCIAL LIFE OF SCHOOL

Before we started the 5-Hour School Week, I was certain that the best and only way kids learned healthy socialization skills was in the school setting. One of my greatest fears was that, if I homeschooled, they would become isolated and strange. As I met actual homeschooling families and read literature, I changed my mind. Little by little, I realized that traditional schools are not only *not* the only way for kids to build their social skills, but they are not even a healthy environment to build on this important skill. Why? Because schools are so completely unlike the real world.

Aaron and I are both from the same small town in Oregon, and we went from preschool and kindergarten through high school with the same set of kids. When we headed for college, it was a shock. Neither of us knew how to start conversations with people we didn't know. "I failed dramatically at college social life," says Aaron, "because, although I was popular in high school, I was a nobody in college, and I didn't know how to start as the low man on the totem pole. I just didn't have the confidence to walk across a room and start talking to a stranger."

In addition, school significantly limits your ability to thoughtfully choose your friendships. You are put in a classroom with thirty kids, and you are told, "These are all your friends, and you will share everything with them and get along. No matter what." When else will that occur in your life? Is it even healthy?

Aaron and I are firm believers in the saying, "We are the sum of the five people we surround ourselves and spend the most time with." We each have about five superinfluential people in our lives, and it's important to us to be incredibly picky about who they are. When someone tells you, "You must be the friend of every person in this room," this priority gets diluted—and it certainly does not mirror real life. In real life, you will encounter people you don't get along with or even agree with—people who live life in an entirely different way than you. We can be kind to and have manners with everyone we meet, but that does not equal real friendship.

School does not teach the vital skill of discerning healthy friendships and how to make choices about who will make up your tribe. School is also only able to supply a limited population of kids, most of whom come from similar environments and upbringings—or from somewhat concerning homelives—making the world our kids live in extremely small and selective.

AGE SEPARATION IS DOWNRIGHT STRANGE

One of the most bizarre social institutions of school is the strict separation by age. Five-year-olds hang only with five-year-olds, ten-year-olds with ten-year-olds, and so on. The only adults the kids encounter at school are teachers, with whom they have a very specific and limited relationship. How does a five-year-old learn to be a ten-year-old if he or she is kept from socializing with ten-year-olds? It's not easy. How does any kid learn about different ways of being an adult or how to *talk to any kind of adult*, if they only encounter that very specific breed, called "teacher"?

Now that we homeschool, I see that daily, my kindergartner learns so much from my first grader, and I see that my first grader learns so much from my fourth grader. It's natural for younger kids to learn from older kids—but school actively prevents that from happening.

It's healthy and natural for older kids to teach younger kids. In the process of being a teacher to other kids, they learn more about themselves, they learn more about their subjects, and they learn compassion. It's a great feeling to have mastered something so well that you can teach it to somebody else.

And doesn't that simulate the world we live in? Age does not define success or capabilities once we leave school. A teacher can present themselves at any age and in any walk of life; a student should be ready to learn from anyone.

CAN YOUR KIDS TALK TO ANYONE?

As we travel and "world-school," my kids have naturally encountered all kinds of adults—from supermarket checkers to police officers—and they're becoming comfortable talking to literally anyone.

In his work, Aaron hires a lot of people, many of them recent college graduates. Time and again, he's amazed how these young adults come to interviews unable to hold a conversation. He says they simply cannot look him in the eye and talk about their lives or their experiences: they look down, or they look at their phone, or they just recite their résumés. It makes him think about the fact that these kids have college degrees—how is it that they aren't capable of chatting with another adult?

What's the problem? Throughout their lives, these kids have been living in the "school box" and they just don't know how to function in the real world. They have had little to no experience carrying on a conversation that wasn't directed by a teacher. Having original thoughts or sharing interesting facts about oneself has not been encouraged. Usually, by their mid-twenties they will realize how crucial these skills are to landing a job and become frustrated that having a college degree will no longer guarantee a career. By that time, it can be too late.

REAL-WORLD SKILLS

Of course, school doesn't just fail to "socialize" kids for the real world. It also fails to teach them basic life skills. No one should reach adulthood without knowing how to scramble an egg, open a bank account, do a load of laundry, use a credit card, jump-start a car, or read a subway map. There's an old gag that goes, "Now that it's tax season, I'm glad I learned the Pythagorean theorem." You may laugh now, but when you were twenty-two, maybe that joke wasn't so funny.

Aaron and I can't believe the number of young people we meet who have no understanding of where the money that their parents use to pay their college tuition comes from, or who graduate with student loans, not realizing they will have to pay them back.

A genuine education should teach life skills, not just academic skills. Despite the occasional and optional "financial management" class, schools generally turn a deliberately blind eye to the real needs of their students.

Recently, Aaron hired a thirty-two-year-old man with a college degree, highly qualified as a construction engineer. When HR asked this man for a bank account where they could direct-deposit his check, he said, "I don't have a bank account. I'll just take it to a check-cashing place." How could this otherwise educated man have reached thirty-two without a bank account? In part, you have to blame the schools. They'd never thought it important to teach him how to manage his money and never explained how that check-cashing business is taking a percentage of the money he works so hard for. An extension of the problem is the outstanding population of young adults with credit cards and zero comprehension of what interest rates are!

CREATING THEIR OWN VICTORIES

In school, kids are responsible for learning their lessons, but they have no freedom or authority to say how they are going to learn. They're told that there is only one way to find a solution, when, in reality, there may be five ways of coming to the answer.

It's important for kids to know that they have something to contribute and that their contribution is important. They should be able to say what's on their mind and ask questions without being afraid that they'll be reprimanded by other students or teachers. Encouraging passionate learning should be the goal, not preparing to pass a mandated, government-enforced test.

"ALTERNATIVE SCHOOLING"

It's beyond the scope of this book to talk about the wide variety of alternative schools now available to parents—such as Acton, Waldorf, Montessori, Play Mountain Place, and the many others.

These programs often improve on the model of school and offer greater independence and lower-stress environments. Often, they try to create projects that imitate the real world—such as creating a profitable business plan and participating in a career fair at Acton Academy.

A big part of building our own 5-Hour School Week has been cherry-picking the parts of these working models that I love most. It's important to really evaluate what is working and what you would want to be different. Before I took the girls out of school, I had a conversation about my internal struggle about school with a friend. She said, "I'm not interested in raising a Harvard graduate. I'm interested in raising a good, kind, God-honoring human being." I never looked at curriculum the same again! What is your goal for your child's education? If it's to get them to Harvard, great! Did you know Harvard accepts homeschooled kids? There is never just one path, so I urge you to explore whether you are on the right path for yourself and your kids.

GOVERNMENT "HOMESCHOOL" TRAPS

When we quit traditional school, we knew we wanted to personally guide our children's practical, real-world learning. Like many beginning homeschoolers, we were first at a loss about how to organize their academic education. We were also afraid of violating the law. So we briefly looked into quasi-government programs, such as the K12 online schools.

We had seen commercials on TV for K12 and thought, *Hey, cool, here's a program that will handle everything for us.* Programs like K12 are accredited by the state and claim to offer a "personalized educational experience."

In some states, these programs not only are tuition-free but even offer stipends to parents who take the role of "learning coach." Very quickly, however, we saw that K12 (specifically in California) was structured exactly like school—with online teachers, grading, and heavy monitoring by the state. The kids would have to clock in to the internet and sit at desks for six hours a day, just as in a classroom. As in school, they would have to "keep up with the class." In other states, such as Florida, the K12 program allows more freedom in regard to scheduling and may not require clocking desk time. Systems like this are better equipped to work with our system.

We saw that if we signed up for such a program, we would be falling into a new kind of schooling trap, and not homeschooling at all. We would not be able to travel as we wished to travel, and we would have no time for all the creative projects we wanted to do with our kids.

REAL HOMESCHOOL OPTIONS

Instead, we started researching the many other educational options available in the modern world: from free learning websites to touring educational exhibits to our own entrepreneurial instincts. We discovered that in our state, as in all the states within the United States, we could homeschool legally just by filing the proper paperwork.

In short, we realized that we did not need to outsource our kids' education to anyone. We saw that we could escape the system—completely. Sure enough, within just a few days of quitting school, we were happily pursuing our own path.

WHERE TO BEGIN

"How do I even get started?" I get asked this question several times a month. The very thought can be incredibly overwhelming, but I promise, no matter what state you live in or what size your community is, there are several options available to you.

After much research on the pros and cons of more organized programs, such as the state-run K12, we filed the needed paperwork to become our own "private school," meaning we are unattached to any one program. By using that wonderful search engine Google, we easily found our state requirements and completed the paperwork, painless and quick.

Here are a few ways we made sure to get connected within our community and incorporate some other alternative schooling options.

Community. We knew we needed a community of friends and parents who lived similar educational lifestyles. I started Googling terms such as "homeschool communities," "local homeschool co-ops," and "alternative education in my area." In our area, we're lucky enough to have a Free to Learn community that focuses on education through play. My girls go there once or twice a week and love it. It also offers me a community of parents and enough support to help me keep from reaching burnout. I encourage you to look into all the options in your area.

Charter Schools. Many charter schools offer a homeschool curriculum. They often provide a financial stipend to help with supplies and extracurricular activities, as well as providing academic and emotional support for any challenges that may come up. Depending on the organization, they may have a very conservative set of rules in regard to attendance and work completed, or may be more lax.

Alternative Schools. We are seeing more and more of these phenomenal choices pop up as well. Alternative schools offer wide varieties of curriculum and educational methods that usually focus on a passion or a principle. For example, Acton Academy focuses on entrepreneurial skills, on learning that grows passion into life skills. These schools vary from city to city, but I encourage you to keep your eyes open. These types of schools are on the rise. Many are really impressive and are a great alternative, but they can also be used in conjunction with homeschool life.

Here are just a few to give you some ideas:

- Acton Academy: entrepreneurship based
- Nature Schools: focus on connection to nature
- Montessori: hands-on learning and play
- Waldorf: similar to Montessori, with more focus on imagination
- Magnet Schools: a free school that focuses on a main technical subject

- Country Day Schools: college prep
- Green Schools: sustainable-living themed

The most important part is knowing what is going to fit your lifestyle best and what is going to work the best for you and your kids. I strongly encourage parents to take time to research and put together a list of several options that might be a good fit. Visit the schools, and if one of them feels right for your family, consider giving it a try.

Co-Ops and Resource Centers. Some of these options can be parent-founded, parent-run co-ops. With these groups, the parents take turns teaching classes in various subjects, both academic and extracurricular. You may also find a privately owned alternative like the one my girls go to. Churches and community centers are often great resources, and many have their own homeschool groups already established.

Asking for Help and Advice. In the beginning, I used social media to find more information. I asked my homes-chooling friends how they and their other homeschooling friends made the options work for their families. I read a decent amount of literature, and I'll share that list of sources with you throughout the book.

While the 5-Hour School Week focuses on educating at home and on the road, I think it's just as important to acknowledge, once again, that this just doesn't work for some families. That doesn't mean you have to sit back and be dissatisfied with your child's education. There are so many alternative school options!

Above all—and I will say this repeatedly—this book is about choices for educating our kids! I simply do not believe one size fits all.

Eager to learn more? Open up Google and start finding what your choices are! And read on—I think we can help a little more. In the next chapter, we'll explain exactly how the 5-Hour School Week works, how we incorporated it into our own lives, and why it works.

TIDBITS AND TAKEAWAYS

- The current school system is based on an outdated system and curriculum that's been used for decades. It was built for a different time and a different world.
- Crowded classrooms lead to a lack of one-on-one time and inefficient use of students' time—the entire class must learn at the pace of the slowest student.
- The school system is getting the best of our kids, especially when you consider that children are at school during the first and longest section of the day, when they are at their best. We parents get what's left at the end of the day, yet we continue to hope for the best part of them.
- While homeschooling is often targeted as not giving kids a healthy social environment, we need to take another look at school's social structure. There's a lack of opportunities for kids to make choices and use discernment when choosing whom to spend time with and build relationships with.
- The skills our children will actually need are not being taught in the classroom. They need to learn practical skills such as financing, intergenerational communication, daily self-preservation tasks, and the list goes on. The simple proof is in the growing presence of "adulting" classes.
- There's a contradiction in expectations: a one-size-fits-all mentality exists in how a classroom runs, allowing little room for creativity or individualism,

yet the pressure to perform is turned up too high too quickly. Let them be little longer.

- If you're noticing these issues, too, and you're considering a homeschool option, take the next step and start reading. There are great books on alternative ways of educating your children:
  - *Free to Learn* by Peter Gray
  - *Most Likely to Succeed* by Tony Wagner and Ted Dintersmith

2

THE 5-HOUR SCHOOL WEEK SOLUTION

I have never let schooling get in the way of my education.

—MARK TWAIN

Freedom! The foundation upon which we've built the 5-Hour School Week. I can't categorize it specifically as world-schooling or unschooling, because it's far more than that. Simply put, it's the way my kids best learn the things we want them to learn, while allowing me to get the best of them: It's taking the travel of world-schooling (because that's our passion) and combining it with independent learning (which some may call an unschooling approach). It's hiking a mountain for physical education as a nature school would, while also encouraging the kids to build their own business as an Acton Academy would. It's taking the concepts and ideas of established systems and implementing them into our everyday life. It's taking what is most important to our family and making it our curriculum. It's a method you can implement, too!

WHY IT WORKS

With the 5-Hour School Week, Aaron and I have found ourselves learning things we never knew or had forgotten since our time in traditional school. More importantly, we're creating special family-bonding moments that reiterate that learning experience. We are learning and creating amazing memories simultaneously!

WHAT'S LOST ON THE "SUPPOSED-TO"S

Freedom also comes from spending time with the kids in the morning, when we're all fresh and at our best—at 10:00 or 11:00 a.m., instead of at 3:00 or 4:00 p.m., when we find ourselves rushing them from school to practices and games.

I know the importance of time. Like any parent, I have regrets about lost time with the kids that I'll never get back. I used to spend a lot of time working, with nannies raising our kids. I didn't realize it then, but they're little for only a short time, and the time is fleeting. Soon, they will be adults with their own responsibilities and their own families.

One of our biggest parenting goals is building a healthy and strong foundation between us and our kids. We want our kids to look back on their childhood with happiness and maybe even say, "Hey, I want to keep hanging out with my parents, because that was great." As parents, we get so caught up in the "supposed-tos" of life. We're supposed to go to college, we're supposed to get married, we're supposed to have children, and the kids are supposed to go to school. With all those expectations to do what everyone else is doing, we forget how important it is for us to be present in our children's journey. That in fact it's our *responsibility* to be present.

Why not enjoy that responsibility? For us, the school system was right in the middle of our family, causing serious discord. The kids knew they would suffer at school if I didn't complete countless forms on time and perfectly. Even helping our kids with homework was creating animosity—and they had homework all the time. Either Aaron and I were not helping them complete the work the way their teacher wanted them to, or we were pushing them constantly to complete their homework so *we* could turn in *our* paperwork. The school system was always present and pushing us into a more discontented life.

THE BEST OF MY KIDS

I'm still surprised at how little I knew about my children when we were in a traditional school setting. Being a mom had always been one of my biggest aspirations, and at that point in life, I was disappointed in what our lives had become. I had joined the rat race of keeping my kids in school, making sure that all their projects were handed in on time, and sticking to all the school's deadlines. I didn't feel like I was getting the quality time with my kids that I, or they, truly needed. I wasn't even getting the quantity of time that I wanted with them. School was getting the best parts of my kids, and I was getting the leftovers.

With our 5-Hour School Week approach, I feel so much more freedom. I get the best of my kids, but my kids also get the best mom I can give them—a mom who is fresh, alert, and present. I used to dread the twenty minutes of required reading every night for our kindergartner, Izzy. By the time I took the kids everywhere they needed to be that day and had dinner on the table, I was too tired to devote that reading time to her—or at least too tired to want to devote that time to her. Now we can sit for a lot longer than twenty minutes in the middle of the day and read together. She reads and sounds out new words, and we're enjoying the learning process so much more.

HANDS-ON LEARNING EFFICIENCY

We've adjusted our lifestyle as working parents so that we work while we're on trips. Our relationship with our kids is so much different—at night, we're talking about what we learned that day. Their school days are the adventures we have together, and we talk about them for days instead of minutes.

I think of it this way: we have to prepare ourselves, even as adults, for transitions. Some transitions are more extreme, such as entering a new country; other times, even the transition from a car to an airplane can be challenging. For kids, transitions can be extra challenging. Transitioning out of an artificial school setting into the real world—which kids who go to school do five times a week—is tiring, difficult, and sometimes just plain impossible. When our kids were living that lifestyle, we weren't living in similar worlds with them. Now we are.

The 5-Hour School Week doesn't have to be an all-or-nothing approach either. Working parents can see similar benefits if their children are in a traditional school setting, too. A visit to Alcatraz one Saturday, followed by a hike at a national park the next Saturday, still creates exciting learning opportunities that families can share together. When we're hiking, it's in the songs we make up or in the book discussions that have nothing to do with the hike that we learn the most. Even sharing educational experiences together just once a month can keep everyone excited and sharing more at the dinner table. Remember that you don't have to overdo the educational elements of activities added to a traditional school experience. You know your kids best. Allow them to learn in a relaxed environment where they are there to enjoy family time and have some fun.

TWO YEARS TO LEARN A LANGUAGE?

When I was in school, I was required to learn a language for two years. I don't remember anything from the French courses I completed. There was a lot of writing and breaking down masculine and feminine—things that had very little to do with actually speaking French.

When we planned our Cuba trip, no one in the family knew anything about Cuba, and we knew very little Spanish. I wanted us all to be able to speak even a little Spanish so we could communicate, learn, and find our way around. Before we arrived, we learned and practiced a couple of new phrases every day for three months. The kids could only handle twenty minutes of new words every day, so we would practice by saying the word, repeating it, and typing it. Using the program Duolingo made this especially easy (and it's free!).

Once we arrived, accomplishing our goals for that first night in Cuba of exchanging our money and finding dinner took us three hours. Driving through Cuba, we learned about the culture—something we all learned together, at the same time, in real time. We quickly realized that just being there and immersing ourselves in the language was going to be the best way to learn. Within twenty-four hours, we picked up four times the amount of Spanish that we had picked up in the previous three months at home.

MAKING THE MOST OF EVERY OPPORTUNITY

Aaron pushed us to take our learning further by asking local people questions. When Maddie wanted coconut water, he told her how to say it in Spanish so she could go negotiate with the vendor for a coconut.

"When someone would fix us breakfast," Aaron recalls, "I would tell them how to say, 'Thank you for cooking us breakfast,' in Spanish, and then the kids would go in and thank them for the breakfast. Once we looked up how to say different words, we each practiced using them, and then we would talk about those things all day long. We reminded each other, 'How do you say *fork* again? How do you say *breakfast* again?' This intentional, in-the-moment learning became fun."

My sister is in the Air Force, and when I was talking to her about our Cuba experience, she told me that the military teaches people languages with the same immersion technique. She's stationed in Georgia, and for much of her work, the people on the base need to know Farsi. She explained that the military sends them to a university in California where only Farsi is spoken, 100 percent of the time, for thirty days. If they need to speak Russian, the military sends them to Russia for thirty days, and in thirty days they speak fluent Russian.

So why do we, in a traditional school setting, spend a minimum of two years in high school learning a language that can be learned and actually retained with a much quicker immersion learning technique?

IMMERSION IN EVERY SETTING

This outlook can be applied to every subject, not just language. Two weeks before we went to the *Bodies* exhibition in Las Vegas, we prepared the kids by learning each day about how the body works in twenty-minute lessons, whether that involved watching a documentary or coloring heart diagrams to learn about blood flow. We woke up every day saying, "We're going to learn about a new organ today" or "We're going to learn about a different bone structure today." Now Izzy can tell you about the four chambers of the heart and how it receives oxygen. Familiarizing ourselves with organs and body systems made the exhibit incredibly engaging for the kids. They would point at a chamber in an actual heart that was on display and say, "Mom, this is the right atrium, like we learned!" After walking the entire *Bodies* exhibit, there was an opportunity at the end to hold a real liver. The girls could not believe how it felt and how heavy it actually was.

Any subject can be learned this easily and quickly with stronger retention for kids when it's learned intentionally. With our approach, kids learn for very short amounts of time, and then the information is sealed with a hands-on, real-world application.

TRADITION OR RE-ENVISION

Traditionally, we equate productivity with time. The quantitative number we can attach to how much time we have spent working on something. A person who puts in at least forty hours of work per week is assumed to be a harder worker than someone who works only twenty, and of course there is always "extra credit" for overtime. The 5-Hour School Week focuses on quality over quantity. There will always be projects and skills that you will only attain with time and practice. However, if we honestly look at how we spend our time throughout the day, can we say we are being our most productive selves? Are we concerned with the quality and understanding of our work or just how much time we've invested in it?

LOSING EIGHT HOURS TO GAIN TWO

In a traditional school environment, teachers are trying to teach eight hours' worth of material in two workable hours. With recess, breaks, lunch, and shuffling between classes, the school day is easily cut down to about four or five hours of actual instruction time. By trying to teach eight different subjects every day, throughout the day, there is a natural fifteen-minute transition period to adjust between subjects, cutting the learning time down even more. At the end of the day, students are lucky to have two hours of instruction time, with maybe even fifteen minutes on each subject.

With so much packed into each schedule every day, how much of that are they even retaining? When do they get to ask questions? What if they already know the material being taught that day? Students risk wasting their time or being pushed at a pace they can't keep up with, and many become afraid to ask questions.

FIVE HOURS MEANS FIVE HOURS

Compare this to a 5-Hour School Week setting: if I sit down and focus on math for one hour on a Monday, we can finish a whole week's worth of instruction in this time. Instead of trying to pack eight hours of schooling into two hours at school, every hour dedicated to learning is used for just that—learning. It's so much easier to concentrate and focus on one subject at a time. At the end of the week, I ask them, "Hey, what do we want to learn next?" We then explore the next subject next week. With this one-on-one learning approach, they learn as fast as they can. If they need help, I can answer questions on the spot, and we move on.

With learning to read, for example, we no longer spend countless hours on flashcards or spelling tests. Now we just learn by reading. We pick out a book appropriate for age and reading ability and jump right in. If one of our kids doesn't know the word, we sound it out together. When they're excited about the story or article, they teach themselves to read faster.

TIME LOST OR TIME LOVED

In traditional school, so often kids are taught something without having the ability to experience it. Then, when they do finally enter the real world, we're confused why they don't know how to do things we were certain they had learned. Even more frustrating is that they are not learning common sense or how to think for themselves in school. Traditional schools tell kids how to learn, even though everyone learns so differently. The girls are each unique in the way they learn and in what helps them retain material. For example, Charlotte needs complete quiet and is very serious when doing work, but Madelyn blasts music in her headphones to concentrate. Their minds just work differently—they require different environments to learn with their own highest efficiency.

The extra thirty-five hours our kids get back each week in the 5-Hour School Week approach allows them to follow their passions and to pursue whatever interests them at the moment. We'll spend weeks reading, building web pages, playing chess, building with Legos, and putting together puzzles. They have the opportunity to spend time on something that truly interests them, and they can start mastering skills at a much earlier age than if they were still in traditional school. The girls love to pass the time by writing songs and singing them to each other— this fun activity covers reading, writing, and creativity. They are learning and aren't even aware of it!

By the end of the week, they've had these focused five hours—equivalent to what other kids are learning in their forty hours at school. Aaron says, "We're doing everything that the other kids are doing, but now those extra thirty-five hours—the time we're saving by them not being at school—become bonus time. This is time to go to parks, to play outside, to have actual, real-life experiences."

The concepts behind our 5-Hour School Week are similar to what Timothy Ferriss discusses in his book *The 4-Hour Workweek*. Ferriss talks about how workplace distractions interfere with productivity in the work day. From distracting emails and social media to coworker conversations and coffee breaks, eight hours at work rarely equals eight hours of productivity.

What about our kids in school? They're at school for eight hours each day.

Realistically, they have the same distractions. They're going from one subject to another. They're hearing a kid next to them ask them a silly question, so now instead of learning long division, they're distracted by other students. We think that if, at the office, you're forced to be reactive instead of proactive, and you're getting only an hour or two of productivity out of your eight-hour day, it is exactly the same at school. It becomes difficult to accomplish what you hope to accomplish.

THE 80/20 PRINCIPLE

Ferriss also discusses the Pareto principle, or the 80/20

rule. So, let's say, in building a house, it may be easy to get 80 percent of the work complete, but the last 20 percent is the most difficult to finish. Applied to the 5-Hour School Week, in an hour of extreme focus and no distractions, kids will learn at least as much, if not more, as what they were supposed to during that entire eight-hour school day. Instead of being distracted, or losing focus, or jumping from subject to subject, students are being taught one-on-one, at their individual level. They work as fast as they can, and they learn as fast as the computer or other programs will allow them. If they have a question, they receive one-on-one help and then they move on.

The Pareto principle—also known at the 80/20 rule—applied to education: 80 percent of what a child learns in school takes place within only 20 percent of the time they are in school.

In a seven-hour school day, a child will spend 2.4 hours learning 80 percent of the material, and the remaining 5.6 hours absorbing only 20 percent of the material.

So if it takes kids an hour to learn 80 percent of what they need, what about the other 20 percent? Is it worth spending six hours to learn that remaining bit? We don't think so. Kids may not necessarily have to learn 100 percent of everything. Much of what we learn in an educational setting is about understanding concepts, but often the details do not apply to real life. Even, for instance, in learning a foreign language, learning 80 percent of that language allows someone to be competent, interact, and frankly, survive.

PREPARED FOR WORLD LEARNING

In Ferriss's *4-Hour Workweek*, with advance preparation, you can work anywhere in the world. We've applied the same concept to our school week—just as any location can be a workplace, any location can also be a classroom. Having Wi-Fi can be handy, but learning can happen anywhere—even if you can't be plugged in—in so many different ways. We use local museums, parks, and exhibits, and we listen to podcasts as well as watch documentaries about local communities.

Ferriss talks about making your traveling workplace affordable, and that's a principle we also live by for our traveling classroom. We've figured out how to travel in a way that's not going to break the bank. Using Airbnbs as well as Airbnbing out our own home has become important in keeping our travel costs down.

PURPOSE AND INTENTION

For Aaron, *The 4-Hour Workweek* was a game-changer. It

changed how he worked and how he lived, and it set an example for our family's lifestyle change.

Everything we do, we attempt to do with great purpose and intention so there is a lot less wasted time in our day. Our life is about living big and full and present. We ask ourselves, "Are we being present in this moment? Are we aware of what we're learning? Are we aware of how we're feeling right now? What are we taking in?" Instead of having the attitude that we *have* to be somewhere and that we *have* to learn something, we ask why we're learning something and why we want to learn it.

We live in this information age where there is so much information coming at us. It's always coming at us through Facebook and Twitter, through emails and news media. Sometimes the toughest part is dissecting what's real and what's not.

That's why in his work, Aaron emails for an hour at a time, then he closes his email, and he tells his employees to do the same. He sets up auto responses for the times he's not emailing, so emails don't pop up and distract him. This way, he's productive with his time.

Learning—and living—in this style allows for more relaxing times as well. We have the ability to build genuine rest and refueling into our schedule. We don't want our kids to think living completely burnt out is healthy either. We get the best of both worlds. When it's time for school, we're intentional about our lessons so that we are productive with that time. After an hour or two of this focus, we're done for the day, and we can go experience the other parts of life. Aaron used to work seventy hours a week. If his phone dinged with the promise of an email, he would respond to that email immediately. I found myself doing the same thing, and so our girls saw their parents prioritizing emails over everything else. We felt like we had to get to that email, or answer that question, or tell someone what to do.

Then we switched our mentality and decided, "You know what? The world can also wait. The world can wait twenty-three hours to hear back from me, because I don't have to respond to every email right this second." We decided that for the one hour of email time we set aside, we would be completely devoted to addressing the email world; after that hour, we would devote our time to other purposeful activities—that had nothing to do with emails. With a time set aside to be plugged in and tuned in to emails, we didn't have to be plugged in 24/7.

Our hope is that now we're teaching our kids different habits from what we had been. The outside world isn't the most important thing in our life anymore, and the girls notice. It teaches them how to prioritize their time, too, which traditional school systems just don't do.

INTENTIONALLY KIDS

"Let them be little." We hear this so often, but when my girls were in school, I had to ask the question, "When exactly do they have time to be little?" There wasn't time for Legos, for imaginary games, or for dress-up. Recess time is short and typically lacks the environment most crucial for true imagination play. They were missing out on so much of this kind of free playtime. When we started the 5-Hour School Week, it felt like that extra time was just giving the kids back a piece of their childhood. I'm usually blown away by what they accomplish in that time. Watching our kids get to just be kids is the biggest gift in this entire journey.

With five hours a week devoted to traditional educational topics, the remaining thirty-five hours are a mixture of real-life experiences and play. Depending on our travels, the thirty-five hours may be spent very differently—the "extras" while we're on the road can be museums and historical landmarks; while we're home, the extras are learning about diving into new topics, building websites, or engaging in a game that typically involves a talent show or singing competition.

When Izzy isn't practicing reading in her extra time, she's

spending four or five hours every day playing and living in a world of imagination. She plays with her dolls, dresses up, spends hours outside...and there's no limitation on this free time. For her age, this type of play is just as important as the business plans Maddie works on in her free time.

Anyone who walked into our house on an average day might think that we just let our kids play all day long. It's true; I do. In those play moments, the kids are learning so much more than they do sitting at the computer, and they're going through their own process of making those lessons stick. Even when Izzy is playing with her dolls, she's often reading them a book that she just learned how to read. She has the freedom to do what she wants with the learning experience earlier in the day—in this example, she uses her imagination and shares it with her dolls. The education the kids receive in the daily one-hour sticks with them much more than flashcards because they have the freedom—the freedom of time and imagination—to learn the way they want.

JOY INVITES LEARNING

When we adopted the 5-Hour School Week concept, one of the first books I read was Peter Gray's *Free to Learn*. The book is based on the premise that free play is learning time. As I mentioned, our daughters go to a Free to Learn community once a week where they play almost all day long, but they play with sewing machines, they play at the creek, they build video games out of cardboard, they write scripts, and they practice directing and acting in plays.

I compare my kids' experience to my own, and I think of when I'm most successful, whether that be in business or in life. I'm my most successful self when there's a certain amount of joyfulness and play in what I'm doing. It's important that kids learn to hold on to that idea—the world will try to convince you that life is not "supposed" to be fun, but I encourage my kids always to find joy in what they are doing, especially in work. We don't "have" to learn or work—we "get" to—and that simple change in attitude can turn a kid who dislikes new learning opportunities into a kid who is a passionate learner.

This individualized teaching eliminates the need to push our students past their comfort level. Learning is no longer stressful, and there's no measurement or expectation for their learning styles. There are no more races; we don't measure ourselves as fast or slow learners. We are simply learning and will continue to learn.

APPLYING THE PRINCIPLES OF THE 5-HOUR SCHOOL WEEK

It's important to understand that you don't have to be

world travelers to make the 5-Hour School Week work. Local parks, museums, and sites can be great for a field trip. Maybe you are lucky enough to live by a national or state park. The beauty of the 5-Hour School Week is that *you* get to fill your "bonus time" however you dream and with the resources you have.

WHEN TRAVEL IS LIMITED

When we first started the 5-Hour School Week, we didn't have a lot of money or resources to make travel a frequent option. We started with camping trips, such as going to Yosemite as a family or heading back to our old hometown in Oregon and pitching a tent at a campground we had gone to as kids ourselves. However, even a camping trip for a week at a national park or a day trip to the closest children's museum provides so much educational potential. We travel more now, partly because we can, but also because we made travel a priority.

"ANYTHING YOU CAN DO IN ANOTHER CITY, YOU CAN DO IN YOUR OWN"

Sometimes all that's necessary is taking a step back to see what is available around you. So often, we forget to act like tourists where we live. If you live in the area where you grew up, it's especially easy to forget to take your kids where you spent time as a kid.

Aaron and I grew up in Oregon near Crater Lake. When we were kids, we used to go to Crater Lake National Park on a yearly basis. For so long, we forgot about taking our own kids there—something that was so commonplace for us was a new experience and a learning opportunity for our kids. Figuring out all the locales and attractions within an hour's drive allows you to plan great day trips that are not available when kids go to school all day. Most cities have history museums and science museums. Many cities are jumping on the children's museum track, which is such a positive contribution to a community.

TURNING ERRANDS INTO LEARNING OPPORTUNITIES

Taking kids anywhere can be a challenge. Most parents I know wait until their kids are in school or with a sitter to accomplish their daily errands. Parents tell me, "No, we don't take our kids to restaurants. It's a nightmare!" It can take twice as long and feel chaotic with kids in tow—I totally get it. I used to avoid taking our kids anywhere, too.

Then I started to wonder if maybe this mentality is part of the reason kids seem less prepared than ever upon leaving their parents' home and entering the world. If being an active part of the grocery-shopping trip or helping fold the laundry was never part of their daily routine growing up, why do we think they will just jump into these things with ease at the magic age of eighteen? If we don't bring them into public places, how can we expect them to learn how to act appropriately and be comfortable in their surroundings?

Grocery Shopping

Let's not forget the importance of incorporating learning experiences into our everyday lives. Something that may seem monotonous, such as grocery shopping, offers a huge opportunity for growth and independence.

One of my favorite activities is having the kids build our menu for the week. Once we've established what we plan on eating, I have them make a grocery list of what we will need that we don't currently have. Then we go to the grocery store, and they do all the shopping. I typically walk around a different section of the store or grab a coffee and hang out with the baby until they've collected everything on the list. We go to the cash register together, but I have them finish the entire transaction. It's important to me that our kids know they are capable of being independent and self-sufficient.

The activity also provides a great opportunity to talk about how much things cost, and how much it costs for our family of six to eat every week. When we go to Costco, we talk about the difference between buying in bulk versus shopping at Whole Foods, and why things cost a little more when they're organic. We discuss where our food comes from and why we would choose to eat organically. We turn over boxes to look at the ingredients, and we're aware of what we're putting into our bodies and how our food is being grown or manufactured.

Banking

As kids, Aaron and I both had savings accounts and were taught to balance a checkbook. This is just not the world our kids are living in, however, and we believe it's vital to teach them how crucial it is to have responsible money-saving and spending habits. Everything is automatic: the moment the kids deposit money in their bank accounts, they can check their balance online to confirm it was processed. I worry kids have a very unrealistic idea of how money is made, how much things cost, and how they are paid for. So, finances are a major part of the 5-Hour School Week curriculum.

It's important to keep modern-day differences in mind when teaching our kids about banking. Banking and bill-paying are so crucial for kids to begin understanding at the earliest age possible. This electronic world where kids no longer understand how to manage money will cause lifelong poor spending habits. Nearly 69 percent of Americans have less than $100 in savings, and the average American household has over $15,000 in debt.[3] These are terrifying numbers! Unfortunately, financial management is a topic barely touched upon in a traditional school—and not until high school, if at all.

Using Money

Our kids understand that money is not free—and that using credit cards is not getting free money. Even in my twenties, I didn't understand this concept, because no one had ever explained it to me. However, my six-year-old knows that borrowing money is not free; if she takes out student loans at some point, she won't be surprised that she has to pay a percentage back.

At restaurants, our kids order their food themselves, and they review the check, because we've taught them that more errors are made in restaurant billings than in any other service environment. They learn about tipping and they are involved in the process. They know how much their activities cost, and they can choose what they want to participate in, based on the cost and how important it is to them.

---

3   Ester Bloom, "Here's how many Americans have nothing at all in savings," CNBC, June 19, 2017, https://finance.yahoo.com/news/apos-many-americans-nothing-savings-145122319.html?soc_src=social-sh&soc_trk=fb.

JOB INVOLVEMENT

We involve our kids in our businesses, too. It's crucial for kids to see their parents earning the money that supports their life. When I used to list homes, the girls would sit with me as I worked, and I explained to them everything people need to know about homes as we were listing them.

Now the girls sit with Aaron in his office while he works, listening to his phone calls and helping him sort the mail. They're able to open the electrical bills, for example, and see how much it costs to provide electricity to our house. They watch him at speaking engagements, and they're able to see that his work and his speeches impact the lives of others—and that this provides for us. When he's working, he's working for our family. We support his extra hours if he needs them, and our kids understand the importance of this.

SERVING AND EXPERIENCING OUR WORLD

Part of our schooling is serving others in various ways. As a family, we work with Compassion International by sponsoring a child. For forty dollars a month, we help provide this child food, water, and an education.

Last year, on Maddie's ninth birthday, she said, "I want to sponsor my own child, and I want to sponsor a little girl who is my age." We explained to her that this sponsorship required a monthly bill. Her response was a presentation of how she would pay this bill: she had written down how much money she would earn from each chore, and her chore money combined with her birthday money allowed her to pay the bill.

She chose to help a ten-year-old girl, like her, from the Compassion International website. Tehansa lives in Sri Lanka, and Maddie sees her as a sister. She writes to her every month, and she prays for her daily. She pays the forty dollars each month by keeping up with her chores. This past October for her birthday, Maddie and I went to Sri Lanka with Compassion International to meet Tehansa.

HOW THIS WORK AFFECTS CHILDREN'S LIVES

As parents, we're incredibly proud of our daughter and her efforts. Even more special was her reaction when we told her she was going to meet Tehansa—she burst into tears and was so grateful for the opportunity. Because she's only ten, we had been nervous that when she opened her birthday gift and read the card explaining her trip, she would be disappointed that she didn't get the gifts she'd wanted. Most ten-year-olds prefer a trip to Disneyland over a trip to a developing country. We realize that by exposing her to Compassion International and having service goals for our kids, we're changing who they are for the better, and, in turn, they want to change the world.

It's so easy in today's society to get stuck in a bubble as you're growing up. Part of our children's education is to understand the different backgrounds people have, the different educations they receive, and the different homes where people live. Our kids are exposed to some friends who live in much bigger houses than our own and who fly in their own planes; we need to make sure they are exposed to the other end of the spectrum, too.

It's easy to sit behind our gate and in the life that we have and forget about people who fall on rough times. Our girls know that everyone has their own story.

SERVING LOCALLY

Serving the local community is a huge part of what we do together as a family. Aaron participates in 1 Life Fully Lived and the Front Row Foundation, we love the Hands and Feet Project, and we volunteer often through our church. We always wanted our kids to serve their community, but when they were going to school, we didn't have the time or energy to make it happen.

During Valentine's Day this past year, I saw an opportunity for us. Our girls were upset that they no longer experience their typical Valentine's Day parties at school with candy and cards, so I thought, *What if we do Valentine's Day packages for the homeless?* Our kids decorated 150 Valentine's bags, complete with nice notes on the front of the bags. We filled them with socks, toothbrushes, and PB&J sandwiches and drove to a downtown Sacramento shelter. I opened the back of the minivan, and from there, the girls passed out bags to the homeless with a "Happy Valentine's Day."

We created a new meaning to the day so that the girls saw how much more important it is to give than to receive. They realized that everyone they gave a bag to that day was most likely otherwise not going to receive a Valentine's card. They thought about how they used to receive fifty cards at school and about how they often just threw the cards away. We saw women with kids, people without the resources to shower, and others who were excited to receive a pair of socks. The day made a huge impact on our girls, and it set them up to appreciate the importance of serving others.

Even during our Cuba trip, the girls were aware of others' circumstances and how they could help. Izzy, our youngest daughter, noticed that just smiling at people made them feel better. Our kids came from the perspective of a private Christian school upbringing in California, so getting them out of that bubble was so important to me. Now

I have the time and opportunity to open their eyes beyond the privileged life we've been lucky enough to have.

As parents, our goal is less about getting our kids into Harvard and more about raising them to be kind, good-hearted humans. To become such adults, they'll have to understand other human situations and view them with compassion and empathy. We try to expose them to that anywhere and everywhere we can. Driving around your own community to see how other people live is important. Volunteering at your local mission and food bank provides an educational opportunity for kids, especially around the holidays. Everyone can learn and teach this lesson at a local level—you don't need to travel to other countries to teach kids what they have, because the reality is, there is always someone who has less and is in need.

ENJOYING THE WORLD

The first time we traveled outside the country was to Canada. Aaron was traveling there for an entrepreneurial conference, and we wanted to turn the trip into a work and family vacation. As we began to prepare for the trip, we learned about conversions that we would encounter abroad, such as using liters instead of gallons, and Celsius instead of Fahrenheit.

When we were in school, we were taught a memorization technique for temperature conversion that wasn't practical or useful. Although we're able to look up the conversion online, Maddie came up with her own formula for converting to Celsius, and we turned it into a game. She was converting the temperatures throughout our trip, for fun.

The scientific conversion of Celsius to Fahrenheit is C X 9/5 + 32 = F: not too easy to do in your head. Maddie looked up a quick "real-world" trick: double the Celsius and add 28. When you do this, the total won't be exact, but it's usually within 2 or 3 degrees of the accurate temperature, which is close enough for practical uses.

So often, we hear people say that a 5-Hour School Week approach would never work for their family because their kids don't like to learn. That's not true. We are all born with a passion to learn and grow. The dislike of school and homework results from that passion burning out after a few years of being stuck sitting at a desk. Think about how many questions a four-year-old asks; our minds are created to ask questions and discover answers. How we answer those questions as parents, or how we guide them to answer their own questions, is what sparks an interest in learning. As soon as Maddie found out that Canadians use Celsius instead of Fahrenheit, she became interested in finding out why they do some things differently and how that benefits them.

Once kids are interested in a subject, it's important to follow through by answering their questions, or having them answer their own questions, in an intentional way. Encourage them to find the answers on their own and report their findings.

Instead of telling our kids what they'll be interested in and what they'll study, we let our kids lead us in their interests. They are truly passionate learners, but they don't like being told what they *should* learn—by doing this, we, in turn, kill their passion for what they're learning. We let them guide us in their interests, then we guide them in finding the answers.

TIDBITS AND TAKEAWAYS

- Immersion education and making every moment a learning moment will have a higher impact in fewer hours.
- Traditional school teaches about two hours of material in the eight hours that kids sit at a desk. An effective education is about the quality of learning, so why put them through an experience that doesn't benefit them intellectually or physically?
- Play is educational! Let them be little! Allow those little minds to create and imagine! Challenge them with projects that encourage problem solving and innovation.
- The 5-Hour School Week is not about traveling or restricted to those who have a ton of money. Your local community and daily errands can provide tons of educational value. Jump on the internet and look for adventures close by.
- Allow kids to work, to know what you do for your job, and when possible, allow them to take part in that. There are all kinds of age-appropriate tasks kids can help with, from organizing mail to helping with checklists to being introduced to new computer systems.
- Service on any level—home, church, or community—is an opportunity for a valuable education and something all kids should feel comfortable doing. Look into local organizations and perhaps think

about what your family could do on an international level.

- For additional reading material, grab a copy of *The 4-Hour Workweek* by Timothy Ferriss and *Free to Learn* by Peter Gray. These books were great resources for us when we first started (and were written by far more accomplished writers than myself!).

TEACHING SO YOUR CHILDREN LOVE LEARNING

Education is what remains after one has forgotten what one has learned in school.

—ALBERT EINSTEIN

There's no better way to learn than by being present, seeing, touching, and especially interacting with the topic you want to teach your children. A lot of parents experience their children, on any given day, coming home from school exhausted and talking about how bored they were. They've lost interest in the subjects before they've even started.

With our girls, understanding what they want to learn about, then pursuing that knowledge in an engaging way, is the very core of our 5-Hour School Week.

STORIES THAT EMBODY OUR LOVE OF LEARNING

Our visit to the *Bodies* exhibition in Las Vegas, as I mentioned earlier, allowed Aaron and me to see just how our daughters like to learn and how they retained the lesson best. The exhibition is a traveling exhibit that features human cadavers. Some have had the organs removed; some have the tendons and muscles exposed. You can see air moving through actual lungs so you can see all the capillaries.

The exhibit shows the difference between a smoker's lung and that of a nonsmoker. The different features of the skeleton are discussed, as well as brain sizes. At the end of the exhibit, the girls held an actual liver while someone explained everything about it.

Our daughters learned so much from seeing and touching actual organs. Everything about the experience was so visual—such as the demonstration showing what happens when food is chewed, swallowed, and digested. Exposing our kids to this exhibit, created by some of the world's leading experts on the human body, was an immeasurable experience.

This exhibit had such a strong impact on our kids not only because of how amazing it truly is, but also because we were able to prepare them for the experience ahead of time. When we told them our plans, they immediately became interested in learning everything they could about the human body before we left.

We learned about the human body in every way you can learn—we did puzzles, watched *The Magic School Bus* cartoon, and consulted the Khan Academy skeletal diagrams. Charlotte and Izzy colored worksheets of blood flow, while Maddie constructed a heart and presented a poster board for her sisters. Our kids cared about how their hearts worked, and why it's important to take care of them. When I was in seventh grade, I could have cared less about learning this same material.

HAWAIIAN ERUPTION

Almost everyone has built a volcano at school with vinegar and baking soda. We did this project, too, in our 5-Hour School Week, but it taught a very different lesson.

Over Thanksgiving one year, we planned a trip to Hawaii. At that time, there was an active volcano—most likely the only time in our lifetime that this volcano would be active. Even though we were traveling to Maui, we knew it would be important to travel to this volcano site on the Big Island

and see it for ourselves. For a week before our trip, we spent twenty minutes a day learning about volcanoes—we watched National Geographic documentaries, talked about tectonic plates, and showed the kids pictures of ash and molten lava, explaining how islands grow when volcanoes erupt.

The Big Island did not disappoint in continuing our volcano lesson. We visited Punaluʻu Beach, also known as the Black Sand Beach, where the entire site was made up of black sand and rock from past volcanic eruptions. We saw a state park with a petrified forest that lava had helped create, and all the trees were encased in lava. We were able to compare different beaches in various stages of volcanic activity and realize that hundreds of years of this activity had created these stages. Four hundred years ago, Maui looked like some of the beaches we saw on the Big Island.

We started talking to locals about the best way to see the volcano. They informed us that to get the best views, we had to go on a four-mile bike ride at night, then hike down to the ocean to see the lava flow. Everyone said it was impossible to do with kids—we did it anyway.

We rented bikes, strapped our kids to bike trailers, and climbed down boulders to watch molten lava crash into the ocean. The experience was as challenging as the locals had said it would be, but the impression it created on our kids was unforgettable.

Even though taking four young kids on a bike ride down a volcano was quite difficult, it taught our kids that it's okay—even great—to push yourself. We hike together often, and hiking, in and of itself, provides important life lessons. Sometimes we have to hike up impressively steep hills to get to the other side and see an amazing waterfall. Sometimes the experience hurts, sometimes it's hot, and sometimes we're going to be frustrated. When we put in the hard work, we see the rewards. When we are our most productive, passionate selves, we function at a higher level.

After our Hawaii trip, we returned home and made volcanoes. The kids loved building with clay and painting. This was a great creative outlet. But when they were done, they said, "This has nothing to do with a volcano." They were right—after all the documentaries, lava beach visits, and biking down an actual volcano, they learned what reality truly is, and it wasn't a science project with baking soda.

SETTING THE TONE OF THE 5-HOUR SCHOOL WEEK STARTS IN THE HOME

Living out the 5-Hour School Week will look different for every family. Children learn differently, they love different things, and they teach each other in different ways. What I hope to open for you in this chapter is a window into our lives, and I hope to show you how this way of teaching our children has worked for us—offering tips and insights on how to adapt it for your own family.

FREE-FLOWING AND FOCUSED

Before the kids get up, I set up our table, which we call the "buffet of learning." On a whiteboard nearby, there is a map of what we are learning that week, based on what they said they wanted to learn. On the kitchen table, there are three laptops set up, as well as some of their favorite workbooks, a bunch of blank paper, sharp pencils, and crayons. Depending on what we're focusing on that week, the tools on the table may change.

It's important to me that our kids are well rested, so there are no alarm clocks. Around 9:00 a.m., the last child gets up, and they all watch about thirty minutes of TV to truly wake up. Then it's time for baths and making breakfast.

There's no rushing around in our schedule. The day free-flows, and we have a very open environment for schedule changes, depending on what the day may bring. Sometimes Maddie will jump on the computer before breakfast so she can research an idea she had the night before. Most of the time, we begin sometime between 9:00 and 11:00

a.m. They are well fed and well rested, and they're ready for their day. The kids let me know what they are going to study, and they jump into it. Even if they don't feel like working on anything, they come back to what we've mapped out for them earlier in the week.

The kids sit wherever they're the most comfortable to complement their learning style. Charlotte loves doing the majority of her work on the beanbag in the living room, although if she's working on math, she is usually standing at a table. Izzy, on the other hand, will sit on the floor.

Because the school hour is during the baby's naptime, I've committed to being very present in the moment during this time. I ask thought-provoking questions, and I want them to tell me what they're learning or how they have come to certain conclusions. The younger kids often need help with math and reading, so I sit with a whiteboard and we work together at first. I show them examples, then they work out the problems or work on the material on their own. Keep in mind, the main goal is that they are independent learners. It is their responsibility to be accountable for the work they do and how much they accomplish.

Sometimes the girls sit for a solid two hours, engulfed in a subject or feeling particularly motivated. Other times, I wait for the energy to change in the house, and everyone decides what they are going to do next in the day—sometimes it's time to switch subjects, and sometimes it's time to go outside and play. Our afternoons vary from day to day. We may go to the park or to the museum, or the afternoon could simply be about running errands or going to the gym.

I don't like a lot of rules or organization around our days, but one of my requests is that there is no mindless screen time. We never have the TV just running in the background, but we do watch documentaries together.

My other request is that, during our intentional learning time, the kids are present in the subject they're focused on. Occasionally they'll say, "Hey, Mom, I can't be present in this topic right now," and that's okay. Part of me—the honest part—wants to push them during these moments and *make* them finish what they started, or *make* them figure out the answer. I don't push anymore. Instead, I suggest that they run around the house, or that they go outside and get fresh air. When they feel they can be present in the subject, I suggest they come back to it then—and eventually, they always do.

Even though I set aside an hour for intentional learning every day, we almost always do more because the kids choose to come back to the material. They enjoy what they're learning.

ACCOMPLISHING GOALS TOGETHER

During our travel days, every day is different, and the lessons vary. While we were in New York, we all learned how to navigate the subway system so we could visit the Statue of Liberty. We woke up with a plan for the day, we showered and ate breakfast, and we figured out, together, the best way to execute that plan.

We were nervous about navigating the subway, but we did, and we walked out feeling triumphant. We each accomplished something we wanted. For Aaron, it was visiting the New York Stock Exchange. The kids asked questions, such as, "What is the stock exchange?" and "What's a stock?" They learned about stocks and about buying and selling companies.

We walked past Trump Tower and told the kids that our country's president lives there sometimes. By the time we reached Battery Park, we were an hour ahead of schedule for our Statue of Liberty tour, so we rode the famous carousel there. The kids loved it. Even that hour spent in the park was a necessary part of our day—we had time to enjoy the scenery, buy a churro, and have some downtime to regroup.

We rounded out the day by visiting Chelsea Market, a place the kids had been dying to see. They watch cooking shows, and they wanted to see where the chefs buy all their supplies. We walked back by way of the High Line, a skywalk two stories above the city that had been an old railway. As the girls pretended they were airplanes and soared back and forth in front of us, we felt complete.

THE INTENTIONALITY OF CHAOS

The lessons for the day, of course, lie in learning about the city and how to navigate it, but we also learn from talking to people and asking questions. We talk to people who can offer advice—for example, rangers in the Junior Ranger programs for the national parks. Rangers have become our teachers during many of our trips. Maddie's favorite question for the rangers gets them talking about their favorite part of the park.

The days certainly look chaotic from the outside, with a baby strapped to my back and our three girls running around. Yet, at the end of every day, when we ask each other what we learned, we have at least five different, valuable lessons that were fun to experience together. Whether learning about how stocks work, or how to hail a taxi or navigate the subway, we learned something from every bit. Sometimes it's learning, and sometimes it's just the experience itself that provides the lesson.

Some may think that their kids would be bored by learning things on a vacation. We set up each vacation—even each trip to the market—with intention and purpose. We talk about what we're going to do, what the experience will be like, and what we want to take away from it. It's important to think about what we want to learn in each moment, whether it's for the kids or the whole family.

We go into each trip with intention, but it's also key that we prepare before we have the educational experience. Watching a documentary about Ellis Island was so valuable before we visited the Statue of Liberty. Even on local trips, such as when we went to Alcatraz, preparing the kids beforehand is so important. Before going to Alcatraz, we watched a documentary about the inmates who'd lived there. The girls learned everything about the Birdman and Al Capone. Once we got there, they were excited to see things they had heard about in the documentary, such as the library where the Birdman used to spend his time reading book after book about his favorite feathered friends.

Throwing kids into what should be an educational experience and expecting them to learn something just by being there defeats the whole purpose of experiential learning. You can't make kids care about something unless you provide the tools and the planning necessary to spark their interest.

MAKE EVERY MOMENT A LEARNING MOMENT

While in New York, we visited the National September 11 Memorial and Museum. Aaron and I have vivid memories of that day; September 11 will always have a huge impact on us. Our kids, though, have no memory or experience to draw from that day. As Maddie was trying to explain to the other kids what had happened, from the knowledge we had shared with her, I quickly realized they needed to see the news stories and the footage to fully understand. We sat on the floor of our Manhattan hotel room and went through a bunch of news footage from that tragic day. Once we arrived at the memorial later that day, the kids were somber. It felt like they identified with the situation and understood its importance and gravity. As parents—and facilitators—it's our job to show them these things and provide the tools and resources to understand the world around them.

QUICK TIPS

Every moment can be a learning opportunity. Being intentional is the key. Prepare for passionate learning by setting the tone for field trips with backstories and activities. Find ways to engage your children, watching for topics and new perspectives that infuse them with intrigue.

LEARNING TIME PRACTICES

Children get excited about different topics at different ages. There's no set age for suddenly wanting to learn about rocks or why flowers have so many colors or what a tiger's favorite meal is. Children simply learn differently and at their own pace and in their own way.

Stuck at a Group's Pace

When there are preestablished checklists for what each grade level should know, these checklists create boxes where we keep our students. Why can't a first grader learn what a second grader or third grader knows if they're ready? Denying a learning opportunity simply because a student may be "too young" can seriously hinder that child's interest in that particular subject, and their learning as a whole.

In traditional schools, a preset format determines how every child will learn, and what every child will learn, despite their style or pace. Teachers are often stuck in the middle of their fastest and slowest students. If they teach to the faster student's pace, the slower student will be behind and will have to compensate with extra homework later. If they teach to the slower student's pace, the faster student is delayed in their learning and not achieving what they could.

Choose a Pace That Matches the Learning

In the 5-Hour School Week, students are constantly moving forward at their own pace, in a one-on-one setting. With my four kids, I see four very different learning styles, speeds, and patterns. While I have one that flies through math assignments, I have another who simply needs more time for these lessons to sink in. I have some who love learning electronically and others who still feel comfortable with pen and paper. I can adjust assignments and environments for each of my kids (not always easily), but there is no way a classroom of thirty can adjust the same way I can to make our children's learning experience as efficient as possible.

While I never set rigorous goals for our kids, goal-setting is an integral part of homeschooling. It gives us the feeling of accomplishment, which is so important. At the moment, we are using a "Goal Crusher" chart—simply a whiteboard with each girl's name. They get checkmarks for each completed assignment, and upon receiving the set number of checkmarks, they are rewarded. Beforehand, the girls come up with the items that will earn a checkmark and those that won't. I also let them set their goal number and prize. For now, this is working, but I know it will need to be switched up eventually. Find what motivates your kids, and help them determine the goals they should be setting for their own life.

We go through the steps of mapping out a learning agenda

on our whiteboard once a week. We figure out what we want to learn and share, and what our days will look like. My role is to organize this discussion and to make sure that every day or so, we're covering math and reading. The other times, the kids pick the topics to study. During Chess Week, Aaron helped with the lessons, which included watching documentaries on chess players and playing chess. During the time we studied anatomy, I bought them a forty-piece skeletal puzzle. Each week, I ask myself how we are going to learn a certain topic the best way.

Once we've completed a particular topic, we erase the whiteboard and start fresh with brainstorming for our following week. Each whiteboard includes individual goals for each child, with their own special project attached. With these individual projects, their general studies, and the theme we're currently studying, our agenda is full.

THE BUFFET OF LEARNING STYLES

Charlotte can't learn math sitting at a desk. Math requires too much concentration for her body to be still at a desk. Maddie learns best while working on a computer, while our younger daughters prefer to write longhand because they're still learning that skill. I find hands-on learning—counting actual coins and bills for Izzy, for example—is much more productive than trying to have her complete worksheets. There are times Maddie has expressed that she just isn't catching on to a concept through her Time 4 Learning program and will ask me to find an additional worksheet or book to try to further explain it to her. We not only all learn differently, but we also process different material differently, and honestly, we don't even know what works until we try something different.

Many people learn and work better in varying environments. One of the greatest benefits of being home to learn is that kids can learn wherever they want, whether it's sitting on a couch, standing at a counter, or sitting on the patio outside. Having the option to be in the best learning environment for each of them is priceless. When they're comfortable, they're willing to put more focus into whatever they're learning, and they're frustrated less by having a less-confining space. They learn faster and accomplish more.

USE ALL THE SENSES

The more interactive the experience, the greater and more lasting the impact a lesson will have. It's about more than seeing. Can they touch it? Smell it? Taste it? Hold it?

When we explore a new area, we love to awaken our taste buds with local famous cuisine. The world becomes learned by more than seeing pictures in a book or on a website.

When we explore museums, national parks, and historical sites, the learning flows into them from every side. The experience of holding a human liver at the *Bodies* exhibition is an experience they will never forget.

When I introduce a new subject, I look up ten different methods for teaching the material. I provide all ten methods to our kids, and when the subject material clicks, I know we've hit the right method for that child. It's very fulfilling to learn about my kids' learning styles, because it allows me to know them on a very personal level, in a way I would not otherwise have known them if I were sending them to school every day. Why is this so important to me? Because knowing how they learn and receive information, and how their minds process helps me teach the other really important lessons—such as manners, kindness, spirituality, and growth mindset.

KNOWLEDGE AT THEIR FINGERTIPS

Our kids are brainstorming new ideas regularly. We can't start a business the second they want to, especially because that's not reality, and that's not how businesses start. When Maddie told me she was ready to start her online baking business, I told her that she first needed to find a business plan and research her target audience. I asked how much money she was willing to invest in her idea and how she planned on marketing the business.

Two hours later, after Googling "business plan," she found a kid-friendly business plan layout. The form had her answer questions and walked her through the process of starting a business. When she had questions such as, "What's a target market?" and "What does that mean?" I'd help her answer them, and she would continue on with her research.

Letting kids have their aha moments, as Aaron likes to call them, is what allows self-learning to flourish. No matter their interests, let them follow and turn those interests into topics they can learn from. The number of resources available today to help kids follow and master their interests is growing by the day! And with so many great tools, there is no limit to what our kids can really achieve.

When I was a kid, I went to the library and used newspapers and encyclopedias to learn. We didn't have YouTubers instructing us on how to do *everything*, from applying makeup to building rocket ships. There was no "instant learning" or instant gratification in the learning cycle. Education was not as easily accessible as it is today.

Today, technology empowers any parent or any child to be an instant teacher. This allows homeschooling to be an option for every family. If your child decides they want to make homemade playdough or sew a dress for their doll, even if you don't know how to make playdough or sew, you can point your child in the right direction and help them find the resources to learn. Even better, you can learn alongside them!

Programs such as Khan Academy, an online teaching resource, have well-educated, phenomenal teachers available at your child's fingertips, ready to teach anything from basic arithmetic to complex equations, for example. Besides the high-quality education they offer, the program is completely free of cost. When Maddie completed an online tutorial about art history, she woke up the next day begging us to visit Paris. She had learned everything about Rome's Sistine Chapel online, and she was not limited in any way—online you can learn anything, at any age.

Part of the value of a traditional school setting in the past was its ability to teach students *how* to learn. When we tell some people about the value of online education, they point out that Maddie would not have known how to self-learn if she hadn't gone to a traditional school first. However, Izzy can navigate online resources to self-learn without having had any exposure to a traditional school environment. The point is, we no longer need to learn how to learn, because it's now a different process.

With a new process comes new challenges, too. We constantly talk to our kids about reputable sources and how to decipher good content from bad content. They are learning the important life lesson of staying on task and how not to become distracted by sidebar ads and videos online. We discuss internet safety constantly. This is an ongoing, ever-changing discussion in our household. Until I feel comfortable with a site and how my kids are using it, it's just not allowed. I ask the girls to show me how they navigate when they are searching for content or ideas. Above all, I am always trying to educate *myself* about the current dangers and solutions in regard to kids and the World Wide Web. There's no shortage of books, parental locks, and information that will help you if this is also an area of concern for you. It's a topic I highly encourage you to take into your own hands and become educated about, if you have not already.

ARE WE LOSING ANYTHING?

I always enjoyed the Christmas pageants and spring performances that Maddie had at her school. She had so much confidence stepping on the stage and singing, and I was her proud mom.

You would think I might miss the official school plays and performances after switching to the 5-Hour School Week. After all, attending them was almost like attending a professional production, and the kids performed so well in them. Yet when Maddie wrote her own script, produced a play, and built the set with all of her peers at her Free to Learn co-op last year, I knew that this educational approach could not be beat.

It was obvious that it was produced by kids—there was no professional, polished feel. All of our girls were involved in the process, and they all were so proud of themselves. They had the freedom to own what they were sharing with us, and they were responsible for the outcome. There were so many skills that Maddie utilized in putting the play together: she assigned parts, she taught others how to memorize their lines, and she directed. All the kids used a variety of skills with the production—skills they could apply in careers down the road.

Even more important, however, is the fact that Maddie produced this play with her siblings and her peers. Eleven kids were involved in the production, from stagehands, who painted and built props, to the youngest kids, who were extras. They needed one another because each of them has a different skillset, but they all have similar mindsets. The experience was so important to each of them. This type of social interaction, where there are few guidelines and little adult supervision, was more valuable to the social development of our kids than the social experience they had in school.

VALUE THEIR INTERESTS, AND LET THEM GUIDE THEIR LEARNING

Kids are passionate learners—more so than adults. They are born with a curiosity to learn that hasn't been tampered with by society. By giving them the freedom to learn what they want, they will learn more and take their learning beyond what you can imagine for them. If they're asking the questions, then they need to know the answers. If something interests them, it's important that they have the freedom to learn about it.

When we set strict guidelines for what kids *should* learn, as in a traditional school setting, we're saying that they only need to learn what we've decided they should. Schools limit kids significantly with these standards. On a recent trip to London, I was amazed at the different topics each girl gravitated toward. It felt like we were on several different trips at the same time. It was so fun to see Izzy become obsessed with the royal family, asking a thousand questions about lineage and heritage. Honestly, I think she is just trying to figure out a way to marry a prince, but in the process she has learned a ton!

Charlotte was in awe of Stonehenge, trying to understand how this mystery has not been solved and how she could go about solving it herself. The architecture of the grand castles really impressed Maddie, as did all the art. If I had limited the material to only focus on the basic history of this incredible country, the girls would have missed the opportunity to find new areas of interest, and we would have learned far less on that trip.

EXPLORING THE WORLD OF ENTREPRENEURSHIP

Maddie has always been good at taking something she loves and turning it into an entrepreneurial opportunity. When she decided to combine her love of baking with a sales opportunity during her sister's soccer games, we fully supported Maddie and her friends in this endeavor. They decided that if they stayed up Friday night after school and baked a bunch of treats, they could pull their Radio Flyer wagon around at the soccer game the following day and sell to the families attending the game. Wearing the personalized aprons they made for marketing, they worked the game for two hours every Saturday for three months. After the game, they evaluated which treats people bought first and liked most. By the end of soccer season, each little girl had made more than $200.

RESEARCHING THEIR PASSION IN THE REAL WORLD

The last week we were in Philadelphia, Maddie decided, during her extra study time, that she wanted to start a new business. She started researching "businesses that children can start" online. Of the ten to twenty options she found, she decided to start a greeting card company.

Later that week, we were at an event for entrepreneurs. While Aaron and I were mingling, Maddie started talking to a group of people about her business idea. Our nine-year-old daughter talked to a group of adults by herself, for twenty or thirty minutes, brainstorming business ideas. She didn't stop there.

During an after-party with friends and future friends we hadn't met yet, Maddie got everyone's attention. With the lights from the rooftop deck shining brightly on her and her notepad and pen, she stood on a chair and said, "Hey, guys, I have something I want to share with you really quick. There's something that I need your help with." She laid out her business plan: a subscription plan where once a day, a week, or month, she would automatically send a greeting card on behalf of a business to a list the business owner provided. With their help, she promised 50 percent off their order, and she asked them questions about what they would pay for the service and what it was worth to them.

She spent the next hour going from person to person, gathering ideas and pointers, email addresses, and phone numbers. By the end of the night, she had twenty new customers and people willing to invest $15,000 in her business.

With no preparation, she stood on a chair, presented a business plan, and engaged an audience of adults. A year before, she had been super-shy and insecure and wouldn't even talk to adults. Now she is speaking to adults like the fellow entrepreneur she is. It showed us the possibilities of this new life.

THE DIFFERENCE THESE EXPERIENCES MAKE

All of our kids now feel, in a respectful way, that they are more equal to adults than they had felt in the traditional school setting. Whereas before, Maddie had raised her hand and asked permission to use the restroom, now she's asking adults advice on her target market audience and whether this service is valuable to them.

Maddie's business proposal acted as the perfect conclusion to an intense week of 5-Hour School Week events for our family in Philadelphia. We did a lot of team building, such as canoe races. Our girls did tightrope walking and ropes courses that challenged them to push through fears of climbing forty feet up trees with just harnesses. They started their days in tears and ended triumphant and proud.

They listened to kids who are motivational speakers speak, and they had the opportunity, all week, to be with like-minded families—families who value a nontraditional school approach.

In a real-world scenario like Maddie's business idea, if the business is successful, she knows that she's done a good job. Business owners will tell her, "Hey, this is going to add value to my business." She doesn't work toward that gold star or the A+; she works toward a paycheck and a successful business idea. If she starts to make less money, she knows that she needs to tweak her business. It's real-world experience, and it teaches applicable, practical lessons. Most importantly for us as parents, Maddie is more excited to work on her business plan than she ever was to work on school projects, because the business is real, and because it matters. It's not a pretend project of a business she might run someday—it's a real business that she can start right now.

THE PARENTS' NEED FOR BALANCE

After we decided to pursue the 5-Hour School Week, it took me a couple of months to figure out a good personal balance so I could be my best self for our family.

THE FEAR OF NO "ME TIME"

I find that the fear of no "me time" is so big that it holds people back from choosing a homeschooling method. Many think that if they choose to homeschool, they will be sitting at their kitchen table for six hours a day with no adult time or interaction—and definitely with no personal time. What separates our method of homeschooling from the traditional homeschooling approach is this self-care philosophy.

For example, during our free time, if our kids are not using this time in a productive way, or if they find that they're bored, I point them in the direction of an inspiring activity. The other day, it was Legos. I asked them to build something innovative with Legos, then write a story about it. During this time, I was able to focus on what I needed to accomplish.

Also, when the kids are studying in the morning for that solid hour or two, I have much more time than I'd originally thought I would, or than many people think they will with instructional time. I can wash the dishes or fold laundry and still be available for questions.

Our focus on self-care is a family focus. Whenever someone is feeling burnt out or lonely, it's important that we express those emotions and talk about them. As a society, we tend to overlook the importance of acknowledging these feelings in the family. I tell my kids when I'm tired and that, to be a good mom for them, I need to take a moment to myself.

Some may find this approach selfish—but it's not. It's good for your kids to see that you're human and for them to see how humans communicate their feelings. Izzy will say, "I'm tired and it's making me feel angry." I know then that a quiet, cool room where she can read a book would be in her best interest in that moment, and she knows she can tell me how she's feeling.

IT'S NOT ONLY ABOUT THE KIDS

At the risk of offending someone, I feel compelled to say this: it's not *only* about the kids! In the first chapter, I wrote a lot about the discontentment of being a mom stuck in the rat race, who not only got the worst of her kids but also gave the worst of herself to her kids. Choosing this journey was as much for myself as it was for my kids, and if you don't learn anything else about homeschooling from this book, please know this: losing yourself in this process will be of no use to you or your children. This isn't about sacrifice; this is about thriving: thriving as a family, learning as a family, growing as a family! So please, please, I beg you—take care of yourself!

FIND THAT ONE THING JUST FOR YOU

I started training for an IRONMAN nine months ago. It's a lofty goal, as I've never been very athletic or a great competitor...and I have no idea when I will cross the finish line. But this goal I've set is mine! I set time aside to train; I educate myself (and I'm learning so much!) about nutrition and how our bodies work. I'm pushing myself, and I'm feeling stronger and healthier.

My point is this: be just as intentional with your time as you are with how you educate your kids. Get it on a calendar and don't cancel on yourself, whether it's training, writing a book, time at the spa or the mall, or having lunch with friends—and don't forget date nights! Challenge yourself the same way you are challenging your children! For me, the IRONMAN gives me something to work toward. It's something I will be able to check off my list, my accomplishment.

TIME FOR YOU

Chances are, you're in or near a community that has social or hobby groups, art and exercise classes, or a number of other opportunities to connect with people, especially mommy groups and parents' night out events.

Think about what interests you, whether it's something you used to love doing or something you've always wanted to get involved in. Do a quick search or ask friends. Take that first step for yourself!

I hired a lovely young woman who loves the outdoors and chaos and is a perfect fit for running my kids ragged two to three days a week for a few hours. It's on the calendar, and we budget for it. This is my time, and it's always after our best hours of the day! I don't give away my mornings with my kids anymore, but I do give away afternoons to focus on myself and what I'm passionate about a few days a week.

I know it can be hard. I know it feels impossible with work schedules and other financial commitments. Get creative.

I promise, if there is a will, there is a way for you to be the best version of yourself and homeschool at the same time.

FULFILLED BY THE RICHNESS OF LEARNING

The personal commitment to, and exhaustion from, homeschooling is what drives many away from the prospect. Truly, my life is richer with our system. I had forgotten how fun learning is. When the girls pick an interesting topic, I'm excited to learn right alongside them. I feel like I'm learning something new every day— and to have this experience with our kids is so important and such a gift.

Mindset matters. I encourage us to think less of "having" to do anything, but rather of "getting" to do everything. When daily errands can be turned into life lessons, we value the chaos of this lifestyle much more and have fun along the way.

TIDBITS AND TAKEAWAYS

- Create your day around a flexible, fluid schedule. Whether it's a buffet of learning like we use or something completely different, keep it simple and practical.
- Stay in that flexible state of mind...always. This will be a process. Some days will feel super easy, while other days you'll wonder what happened! It's okay to change it up as needed.
- Ask your kids the question, "What do you want to learn?" Their interests will guide their learning.
- The education we had as kids does not fit the world our own kids are growing up in. It's okay to be different. Let them know they don't have to have the approval of others before they find ways to love what they learn.
- Take care of yourself. Be a passionate learner. Make a new goal. Go on more dates. Be the best version of yourself so your kids know exactly what that looks like!

GIVING YOUR CHILDREN A (BETTER) SOCIAL EDUCATION

Friendship is the hardest thing in the world to explain. It's not something you learn in school. But if you haven't learned the meaning of friendship, you really haven't learned anything.

—MUHAMMAD ALI

People believe many myths about the social pitfalls of homeschooling. They fall into the trap of thinking homeschooled kids grow up weird or that they won't get enough social interaction. Another is that homeschooled kids won't develop the same long-standing friendships that kids in traditional school do. In reality, this just isn't true. Our daughters have developed many friendships through the various groups they participate in, and their best friends are part of the entrepreneurial group we meet up with occasionally in various states.

THE IDEA OF "HEALTHY"

The number one question we're asked about the 5-Hour School Week, even among family and friends, is, "Aren't you worried about your kids having friends?" There is a general societal stigma that homeschooled kids tend to lack "normal" social skills and are "strange" or antisocial.

Aaron and I both come from families with strong public school backgrounds. Aaron's mom has been in education for forty years, working her way up through the public school system to become a superintendent. My mom recently retired after thirty-five years as a junior high school teacher. There was definitely concern expressed about our kids not having a healthy social environment because of our choosing to homeschool. Forty years of experience has shown our mothers that kids develop all their social skills in the classroom, but I have come to reject the idea that what we have always done is necessarily the healthiest choice.

WHAT TRADITION SAYS

Unfortunately, we live in a society that screams at us to just fit in! Go along with the crowd, don't make a lot of noise, and just do what everyone else is doing. It's what has always been done, so, obviously, it must be right. There was a time in history when class sizes were smaller, school days were shorter, actual play and creative time was ample, and this type of classroom socialization made a lot of sense. That's not the environment our kids are learning in! But because your grandparents went to school, and your parents went to school, and you went to school, it is easy to assume that putting your kid in school is exactly what you are "supposed" to do because it's the "safest" and "healthiest" choice. For some, this may be 100 percent true, but it doesn't have to be the only way.

Before we started homeschooling, of course, this was also one of my biggest worries. I thought that our kids wouldn't have the same experiences I had growing up. Aaron is nostalgic about having the same friends all through school and about the Friday-night football games. He used to brag about graduating high school with the same twenty kids he met in preschool.

In traditional school and in popular thinking, there's an idea that hanging out with the same group of people for twelve years is socially healthy. Whether people had a positive or negative experience in the social world of their school, they see it as a necessary experience. No one considers the artificial nature of the environment created within a school, or how it's nearly impossible to learn the skills necessary to meet new people.

While the choice to homeschool is different from the system most people are used to, that doesn't mean it's unhealthy. When researching traditional school and homeschooling socialization, I found articles about military and missionary families the most interesting. In conversations with those in the military and my worldly friends who have traveled extensively, they often speak of a pattern among kids who have moved and switched schools every few years because of their parents' service jobs. These kids are typically socially superior to the traditionally schooled kids. These kids in ever-changing lifestyles find making and building relationships easier, tend to be more flexible in their thinking, and are actively outgoing to build new friendships. This shocked me! I had always believed the opposite—that staying in the same school environment with the same kids was going to have the best impact.

UNEXPECTED CRITICS

Recently, Aaron had an experience that opened our eyes to the challenges parents face when they pull their kids out of school. He was going to an entrepreneurial retreat for fathers to discuss various parenting methods, and he picked up a group of fellow fathers going to the retreat at the airport so they could all ride together. Because this was an open-minded group of guys, Aaron was surprised when he and another homeschooling dad found themselves defending their choice to homeschool to several other fathers who felt we were providing our kids with a deficient social education.

Reactions like that are hardly surprising to us anymore. Shortly after starting our 5-Hour School Week lifestyle, Aaron had a longtime friend, someone he looks up to, show up to a weekend BBQ but without the rest of his family. Sincerely concerned, he pulled Aaron aside to make sure we hadn't joined a cult or something. After being confronted with this concern more than a couple of times, we realized that people think of cults when they think of homeschooling. It's yet another stigma and one that makes us laugh and roll our eyes. The truth is that our society still holds on to this heavy concern, although the situations in history in which homeschooling was associated with cults were few and far between—and this is definitely not the course homeschooling is on today.

THE FEAR OF "WEIRD"

Whether the topic comes up in a conversation with strangers or longtime friends, it is no secret that one of the biggest fears in homeschooling lies in the fear of what is socially considered weird. Homeschooling is different and unknown—it's strange and so, obviously, weird. While people widely accept that kids can learn on their own, they struggle to believe they are capable of adjusting to different social settings, which is a form of learning in itself. We honestly just don't give kids enough credit.

Even discussions with family can be hard. After not hearing from his cousin for a few months, Aaron received a phone call of support and confession. It wasn't until his cousin saw our Facebook posts about our experience in Cuba that he realized the education we were giving our kids could actually be just as good as, if not better than, a classroom. He told Aaron he felt bad; up to that point, he'd believed we were being irresponsible in denying our kids this same social experience in school that they had had together as kids. Those calls and emails—when people are able to wrap their minds around the fact that different doesn't equal bad—are my favorite.

What Does "Enough" Mean Anyway?

"You don't want them to be weird homeschool kids, Kaleena," my dad will say. "Do you remember that kid who came into junior high after she'd been homeschooled, and how odd she was? You don't want Madelyn to be like that."

I'll reassure him by telling him that Maddie is taking Tae-kwondo, or that Charlotte went to the co-op that day. The response is always the same: "Well, that's good, because they need to be with other kids."

There is always an underlying concern that our kids aren't getting enough social interaction, and that they're going to turn out strange and different. The fact that this is a number one priority is funny to me. We beg our kids not to be followers, but then fear the possibility that they may do anything different than what everyone else is doing: "Be yourself, as long as it fits with what's socially acceptable." A bit ironic!

QUESTION WHAT "HEALTHY" LOOKS LIKE

So I'm just going to ask (knowing that many of you aren't going to like this question): "Are you sure that your children's social environment in the traditional school system is a healthy one?" We challenge the traditional thought process by asking others to look at their own world to see if it is actually providing the social foundation they want for their kids. Yes, there are lots of kids at school; therefore, your kid will be surrounded by a large number of people. But do we measure healthy in quantitative terms or in terms of being toxic versus nontoxic?

Rather than automatically assuming that homeschooling families are doing something socially unhealthy, we encourage families to ask themselves, "Do we have a healthy social environment in place for our kids?"

The media paints a happy, positive traditional school environment—one that we all know can be far from reality, especially for junior high and high school kids. And while I'm no expert, it doesn't take a professional to see that kids are stressed out. They are acting out in ways we have never seen historically, falling to pieces under the pressure of social expectations and in the spotlight of social media. Being a kid just isn't as easy as it used to be.

DOES MY CHILD HAVE HEALTHY RELATIONSHIPS?

What traits should you look for in your child's relationships to know they're healthy?

Talk to your children. Ask what they talk about and do. Do their stories reflect behaviors of trust, compassion, respect, acceptance, and reciprocity?

Take time during dinner, on the drive home from school, on the way to practice, or any other opportunity to learn about your child's relationships.

Even with all the negative assumptions and judgments, it's much easier today to adopt an alternative schooling approach than it was twenty years ago. This is partly because technology allows for an array of educational formats. As alternative education becomes increasingly common, the transition to having a more open mind will hopefully become easier for people.

We've had many teachers tell us that if they had the means to educate their kids the way we do, they would homeschool instead. In talking to teachers, it's funny to hear them agree about the social dynamic of their classroom typically being the biggest obstacle they have to face. In fact, my first fan letter was from a teacher who said that she follows my blog and that our approach has inspired her to change the way that she teaches in her classroom. That letter made my day.

TRADITIONAL-SCHOOL SOCIAL CHALLENGES

Maddie recently had her tenth birthday, and to celebrate, we picked up her two best friends from school. We went out to lunch, and Maddie got her ears pierced.

Buddies since kindergarten, these three girls hadn't missed a birthday party or playdate in years. They are the Three Amigas! I got along well with their mothers, and I really thought we had hit the jackpot in Maddie's social experience. These were her BFFs. To me, it only made sense that they would stay that way forever. However, at the birthday lunch, there was tension between the friends, Stephanie and Lacey. I could definitely feel a competitive tension and was bummed that they seemed to be truly frustrated with each other. Both Maddie and I were saddened by the situation, because they used to be the very best of friends.

That night, I called Stephanie's mom. I described what I had observed that day and that both Maddie and I had noticed that there was a lot of tension between the other two girls. Stephanie's mom explained that it had been a rough year for both girls at school. They had been singling each other out and competing over grades. Feelings had been hurt from bragging and just some not-very-nice behavior. It was clear the situation was making Stephanie sad and withdrawn, so I suggested that maybe she spend more time with Maddie on the weekends and outside of school and that she branch out and make some new friends.

"Yeah, but they've been friends for so long now, Stephanie doesn't know how to make friends with anyone else," her mom explained. "Everybody else has friends, so it's not like she can just change groups in the fourth grade. Not to mention she still has to see Lacey every day at school, so hopefully they work it out."

I remember feeling exactly the same when the girls were

in school, and it makes me so sad! Our kids are not being given the freedom to build their social circle. Instead, they are often obligated to be friends with whomever they're on the playground with, not based on character, similarities, or passions.

Both moms are smart women, and both families are good people. It doesn't seem fair that one mom felt that her daughter was obligated to stay friends with someone who didn't treat her right, feeling there were no other options. While I know we will have our own social challenges and growing pains because it is simply a part of life, I feel great relief in knowing we have many choices. We realize choosing our social circle should be done with great intention.

SOCIALIZING AND HOMESCHOOL

After the kids spent their first couple of weeks attending the Free to Learn co-op, Izzy came home and told me, "You know, this girl isn't very nice to me, and she's not a very good sharer. So I just told her, 'I really don't like the way that you're treating me, and I would rather not play with you today.'" At first, my old thinking jumped right into action with my typical lecture about how she needed to be friends with everybody. I stopped myself, though, and said, "Well, how did your facilitator handle that situation when you weren't getting along, and how did you come to a solution?"

I was so proud when she responded with, "You know, Mom, not everybody is going to be my best friend, and I don't always have to play with everyone. We are all okay with that."

Even at six years old, she realizes that she can choose whom she associates with, and she can find a different friend. In a public school setting, that's not something you can do. It's okay for Izzy to acknowledge that the two of them weren't playing well together and that they weren't going to be best friends. It's important that she knows she can—and should—invest time in a relationship that will be a good friendship.

SOCIALIZING ON THE JOURNEY

We notice the girls showing good social skills on the road, too. Our kids try to make friends wherever they are. We first noticed this when we were vacationing in Hawaii. At the beach or at the pool, if there was a kid nearby, they would ask if they wanted to join in whatever game they were playing. Sometimes kids would be too shy to play, but most of the time the other kids were excited to make new friends, too. Before we knew it, there were six or seven kids playing a game of Marco Polo, making up songs, or choreographing a dance for hours. When it was time to head up to our room for the night, the kids would say goodbye with, "Okay, tomorrow—same time, same place." When we're somewhere for a week or two, the girls end up having friends, and activities planned with them, for a good portion of the trip.

Their ability to make friends so quickly is a direct benefit of homeschooling. Our daughters spend more time together than with anyone else, and they don't have a set group of friends like they would in school. When we go somewhere, they have a hunger for meeting new people that allows them to work through any fear of introducing themselves to new friends. Even as adults, Aaron and I still struggle with going up to new people and introducing ourselves right away. We didn't learn that skill within our secure group of friends. Our kids are able to do this more quickly and more easily because they're learning to do so at a younger age.

INTENTIONAL SOCIALIZATION

Making sure your children are socialized is as simple as taking them with you to the grocery store or bank. I take our kids with me everywhere. We go on hikes with other families, and when we're at the museum or even walking down the street, we meet different people. It's important to challenge kids to not just be there—wherever they're at—and to communicate with them about being involved in the situation.

THE SKILLS WE NEED FOR SUCCESS

As a society, we don't emphasize enough the value of holding eye contact, or asking questions, or answering questions appropriately. The abilities to ace a test or follow instructions are typically not qualities listed in describing the successful; however, effectively being able to communicate with others is always at the top of the list.

That's why we challenge our kids to be actively involved. When we're at a museum, we encourage the kids to ask questions about the exhibit. Or when we're at national parks, the kids ask the rangers questions for their workbooks. When we're at restaurants, the kids order their own food. We know thirteen-year-olds who still cannot order their own food from a waiter or waitress. So much socialization is based on the ability to make eye contact, speak clearly, and not be distracted by phones, menus, or whatever catches your attention when you're speaking.

Being social doesn't just mean being able to play or communicate within your own age group. As adults, we need to be capable of interacting with all ages, from a one-year-old baby to a ninety-year-old grandparent. Why do we judge our children's socialization ability strictly on how well they play with other kids in their class?

FUNCTIONING IN ALL EXPERIENCES

In the same way that kids are passionate learners from the day they are born, play, especially with kids in the same range, comes naturally. It doesn't take long for a group of six-year-olds on a playground to start a lively game of tag, even if they have never met one another before.

Regardless of the environment, kids just know how to meet other kids at the park, or at the pool, or at the museum. Six-year-olds, for instance, know how to play with other six-year-olds. Just because our kids are no longer playing with the same kids at school, day in and day out, doesn't mean they'll forget how to play with other kids their age. What kids really need to learn is how to comfortably communicate with people outside their age group. By exposing our kids to enough experiences, we ensure they'll have a normal, healthy socialization that asks more of them than what is asked of kids in traditional school.

Kids need to be part of larger groups and to understand the feeling of inclusion that comes with that. When we decided to homeschool, we knew we needed to provide that intentional social interaction.

We choose youth groups and playdates where the kids will have fun and enjoy being around other kids. The kids are included in selecting what they do and whom they spend their time with—they have to be a part of this decision-making process. We can understand and respect that our kids don't "click" with everyone they meet; however, kindness needs to be a priority for children as they decide how to treat each other. It still amazes me when I see the girls reach out to someone they've expressed frustration with previously. I have watched the girls, on countless occasions, include other children who have been mean and hurtful to them. When we talk about this, I am impressed with their view. They have the freedom to carefully and intentionally choose the people they spend the most time with, which makes accepting and tolerating those who are harder to get along with less difficult. It's about setting the right expectations going into each social situation—distinguishing your actual "tribe" from acquaintances.

TECHNOLOGY OFFERS MORE OPTIONS

For us, because we're traveling often, exploring all the group options available to the girls is difficult—consistent attendance is not always an option for our family. That's why technology has also enabled our daughters, especially Maddie, to communicate and socialize. Maddie has an email address now that she's ten, and she emails friends and family members often. Technology such as email, FaceTime, and even certain Xbox Live communities—with proper supervision—add to socialization options. Most importantly, technology helps kids choose their friends by preference instead of proximity. In Haiti, Maddie met a sweet girl from Louisiana. With no internet as a distraction, they bonded quickly while making beaded necklaces. They went to visit a local children's village where orphaned children and their caretakers lived in close-knit communities. These villages allow displaced kids to experience a family-type relationship structure. It was a place where Maddie and her friend could connect and share joy with children from different backgrounds.

The girls keep in contact through email, and I have a feeling those two are going to meet up again somewhere really amazing! It's these types of relationships we hope our children build: meaningful, authentic, loyal friendships with people who share common aspirations and passions.

THE BENEFITS OF THIS ALTERNATIVE STYLE OF SOCIALIZATION

Recently, our daughters attended a church camp. When we picked them up, every one of the camp leaders commented on how mature and outgoing our daughters were. They interacted, they participated, and they loved being part of the group.

We hear this often about our kids, and it makes us proud.

We want them to have a voice and to use that voice. I'm around some kids who still look at the ground when I ask them a question, or they look at their parents for an answer. It's always been important to us that our kids are comfortable—and confident—talking to adults.

A CONFIDENCE THEY NEVER HAD BEFORE

We noticed the biggest difference in Izzy, socially, once we changed the kids to our 5-Hour School Week. She used to be very shy. Always looking down when adults, including family, spoke to her, she never made eye contact and would simply refuse to answer questions. Now, at just six years old, she's a leader in several of her groups, she confidently orders her food at restaurants, and she knows to shake hands and look someone in the eye when meeting them. We hear from her group leaders and facilitators that she's one of their biggest helpers and contributors.

A DEEPER CONNECTION

Our girls are definitely still kids. They can bicker like siblings do, overreact, or get embarrassed around others easily. I'm not talking about perfect little angels who speak when spoken to and never tattle. But not only have our relationships with the kids improved immeasurably with homeschooling, we've also seen their relationships with each other deepen. Instead of just sharing a house at the end of an exhausting school day, they enjoy one another's company, treat each other better, and are building some epic memories together. It's important to create space for each of them to have their own experiences, of course. No kid likes spending 24/7 with their siblings, but I love how much stronger the foundation of their relationship has become in the last few years.

LEARNING TO DISCERN THEIR INFLUENCES

My hope for our kids is that they will be able to discern who their cheerleaders are, as well as those who don't have their best interests in mind. At thirty-five, I feel like I'm just getting the hang of it. I struggle with finding friends who share similar values and interests, and I still find it difficult to distinguish a healthy friendship from an unhealthy one. By the time they are my age, I hope our kids have that figured out. I hope they're able to find people who are sincere, authentic friends.

Jim Rohn's famous quote, "You are the average of the five people you spend the most time with," has become so popular in recent years that people are choosing their top five, left and right. They're being selective about whom they spend time with, but they're forgetting that this idea applies to their kids as well. Adults and kids alike are influenced by the people they spend the most time with. If you are constantly surrounding yourself with negative people who only see the glass as half empty, then I guarantee it is only a matter of time before you, too, start to believe in the emptiness of that cup instead of the fullness you saw previously. It's why we tell our kids not to hang out with kids who smoke or drink. We fear that the peer influence will persuade them to partake in the same toxic behavior. We know the habits and attitudes of those we are with the most will have a direct influence on our behavior and actions. As an adult, I choose to invest my time with people who are positive, motivational, and seek to inspire. These are qualities that I want to build in myself, and I know spending time with these types of peers will bring out similar strengths.

DEVELOPING MATURITY AND COMMUNICATION SKILLS

Aaron frequently takes Maddie with him to lunch with other adults. While he's talking to one person, Maddie has no problem talking to the other adults at the table. It's not unusual for Aaron to hear at the end of the meal, "It's amazing that your daughter can just sit and have a conversation with us." They're impressed that she can talk about books she's reading or things she's writing and that she can hold interesting conversations with adults.

It's equally impressive and important to us that Maddie not only can answer questions but can also be just as interesting in conversation as any adult. Let's be honest, this kid has a pretty cool life. She sees some neat stuff and is just as fun to talk to as anyone twice her age. When kids feel comfortable in social situations, it's really incredible to hear some of the stuff that comes out of their mouths!

QUICK TIPS

Challenge your kiddos to order their own food the next time you take them to a restaurant, engage in a conversation with the grocery checker, or approach a new friend while at the park. Give them opportunities to expand their comfort zone, and then watch how they grow. The more you present them with new situations, the more comfortable they will become in them.

We've had some encouraging compliments: "I have to tell you, your daughter speaks to me better than my college-aged son who's going to MIT. She knows how to answer a lot of questions that my son wouldn't even answer. I just had to tell you that you're doing a phenomenal job." Hearing such high praise about Charlotte as we got off the park tram in Zion National Park sure felt great. There wasn't room to all sit together on the bus, so our then-seven-year-old bravely elected to sit toward the front of the bus with a nice guy and his teen sons. It was about ten minutes before the next stop, and I could see her talking this guy's ear off the entire ride—at one point, even opening up her park book to show him the scavenger hunt she was on to get her Ranger badge. I just love this about our kids: they not only love learning something new, but they love sharing and teaching just as much!

CONNECTING ON NEW LEVELS

There's so much value for our kids in knowing how to interact with people from all backgrounds. On a beach in Maui, the girls were running back and forth from the water to a spot they'd set up with all their sand toys. About ten feet away, sitting in the part of the sand still very wet from the waves, was an elderly man. He was using a method to build his sandcastles we had not seen before. With no buckets or shovels, he layered really wet sand, patting it down and then adding another layer, creating beautiful castles!

The girls inched closer and closer to him, until finally they were sitting right next to him. They asked him how he was making the sandcastles, and soon he was showing the girls how to do it. They sat for two hours with him, building sandcastles and talking about their lives. As we packed up the beach bag and chairs, the girls rushed over to share all they had learned from the nice "grandpa" from Canada. They couldn't wait to tell us about his two daughters, one a lawyer and the other a doctor. He had told our girls how he'd taken them around the world and taught them how to build sandcastles just like this. He commended us as parents, that we were giving the kids a "real education," and he was impressed with all they had shared with him.

At every beach that we visit now, the girls use his method to build their sandcastles and we usually talk about the nice Canadian grandpa.

A conversation and the memories built on the beach that day will stick with the girls forever. If they'd only learned how to talk with kids their own age and not built the skills to connect with people of all ages and backgrounds, those moments never would have happened. Our girls would have been sitting in a classroom, not exploring the world and the people around them.

TIDBITS AND TAKEAWAYS

- Healthy socialization is not measured in quantitative value but in terms of toxic and nontoxic. Ask yourself honestly about the environment your children are in every day.

- Kids should be encouraged to socialize outside their age range, building confidence in speaking to people of all ages and backgrounds comfortably.

- Different doesn't equal bad or weird. Let your actions and encouragements for your kids match your words. Don't restrict them to what's socially acceptable; instead, allow their individual voices to be heard.

- Everyday errands provide opportunities to socialize. Take your kids with you so they can learn the skills they need to function in various situations.

- The social environment and needs of our kids today are different than those we had in school. Kids need to explore the many options available for social interactions.

- "You are the sum of the five people you spend the most time with" is just as applicable for children as it is for adults. Allow them to play an active part in choosing whom they build friendships with.

HELPING YOUR CHILDREN ENJOY PHYSICAL EDUCATION ON A NEW LEVEL

Just living is not enough. One must have sunshine, freedom, and a little flower.

—HANS CHRISTIAN ANDERSEN

I hear it all the time: "I can't get my kid to go outside."

Or, "How do you get your kids to hike for ten miles? My kid hates being outdoors."

The obvious problem is that our kids aren't allowed to be outside as much as they should. Kids just aren't as interested in exploring and adventuring outdoors because, when it comes to outside play, they are typically limited to less than an hour a day. And it's limited to guided activities (four square, basketball, and so on).

For our family, physical education is about embracing our surroundings and making every activity an adventure.

COMPETING WITH THE ELEPHANT IN THE ROOM

It's hard to compete with the elephant in the room when it comes to physical education: media, technology, iPads, phones, gaming systems, apps, and televisions! Kids today are addicted to the high frequencies and noise, to the allure of watching a story instead of imagining one. Most American parents experience this constant struggle to coax their kids to get off the screens and get outside.

Kids are used to being inside because, at school, they sit at a desk all day. Recesses are shorter than ever, and physical education has been cut to the bare minimum. Kids are used to being stationary ten months out of the year. With the exception of organized sports, the amount of time kids spend outside continues to decrease, and the amount of time they are plugged in is continuously increasing.

GET INTENTIONAL ABOUT PHYSICAL EDUCATION

Physical education for kids has to be incredibly intentional. The goal is to establish healthy habits in childhood that lead to a lifetime of healthy habits. We want them to be able to carry their active lifestyle into adulthood.

Hiking is an activity our whole family enjoys, and we hike all the time—at home and on the road. You have to be very intentional about hiking with four kids, simply because it's so much work just getting them prepared. After completing thirty or forty hikes over the last two years, I've learned that the most important first step is setting expectations for the experience.

PE RE-ENVISIONED

The world of physical education is not limited to what PE teachers decide in a curriculum. Outside of the school walls are boundaryless activities. Give yourself and your family room to explore. Here are some places to start:

- hiking/running
- rock wall climbing
- paddle-boarding/surfing
- martial arts
- skiing/snowboarding
- skateboarding/ripsticking

- bike riding
- rafting/sailing
- athletic teams: soccer, baseball, football, track, volleyball, basketball, and so on
- skating/ice-skating

I tell our younger kids days in advance of a hike to prepare them. We talk about their being able to bring their special backpack and their hiking stick, and about what the day will be like—it might be a long, hard day, and we're going to have to work at it, but we're going to see cool places and meet cool people. What started as taking half-mile hikes has built, over time, to being able to complete ten miles. At the end of each hike, the kids are always so proud of themselves. It's the best physical exercise for them, and they see so much of the outdoors.

EMBRACE THE CHALLENGES

Hiking is a great experience, especially when you are on the hunt for treasure! A gorgeous waterfall, a hidden water hole, or a spectacular view is usually just the right motivation for digging in deep and overcoming the challenge.

We encourage with fun little contests along the way, competing for the title of "most positive hiker," "fearless leader," or "park ranger extraordinaire." Now, when we travel, our kids look forward to visiting places we've hiked before. The hiking portion of each trip stands out as a point of excitement and anticipation and allows them to make these long-lasting memories.

LET THEIR INTERESTS INSPIRE ACTIVITIES

Let's be honest—not every kid dreams of hiking or gets excited about waterfalls. Izzy, for example, would choose playing with her dolls or playing on her iPad over an adventure through the woods any day. But call her the "leader" while on the trail, and that girl is no longer bothered by her surroundings in nature. She has a special hiking stick and has found that making up silly songs along the way makes the time pass faster.

During a big group hike we were on with other families, Izzy was lagging behind and making it clear she was not loving the entire experience. I hiked with her at the back, and we talked about everything and anything. She made up funny little songs about her sisters and camping. We joked and laughed for a full five miles. It was nice to have that one-on-one time with her, and it allowed her to focus on something other than the hike she was struggling with. At the end, Izzy had the satisfaction of knowing she had worked through something difficult for her and that she did it well. She talks about that hike particularly often—it's a great memory and was physically challenging.

Sometimes, the girls will even surprise us. We had been building our hiking endurance over the course of a year, and I was excited and a bit shocked when Maddie came to me with an idea. The Travel Channel is a favorite in our home, and one afternoon she had seen an episode on secret swimming holes in an incredible place in Arizona. She said you hike ten miles into a part of the Grand Canyon, and there are waterfalls the color of ice-blue Gatorade. She was fascinated with Havasu Falls and was intrigued with the Havasupai tribe that has their reservation at the falls. With a little research, and after convincing a few other brave mamas, we found a guide to lead us on a three-day adventure to Havasu Falls.

I had never done anything like this, and here I was about to go without Aaron on this incredible hike, but I knew that if I fed this passion of hiking, of being an explorer and craving adventure, our children would have awesome lives and become awesome humans! So we planned everything out: we were going to backpack in and spend two nights there, experiencing everything the waterfalls had to offer. Round-trip, the hike would be thirty miles, and a great deal of it was a bit dangerous, especially with three nine-year-olds in tow.

Thinking back on the morning we began our descent into the canyon, it still feels surreal. The sun was just starting to rise as we climbed out of our guide's van. I was speechless at the land that lay in front of us. It was a bit chilly, and we had all dressed in layers. It was a long day, with ten miles of hiking through canyon and desert with three little girls. I asked myself several times, "What was I thinking? How are we going to pitch tents and keep everyone safe?" We were hiking into the middle of nowhere, and as the hours passed and the sun started to get low, I became nervous that I had possibly bitten off more than I could chew.

Just as I was about to go into a full panic attack, we came to a viewpoint, and there it was. The most magnificent waterfall I think there is in the world! The most beautiful blue, so powerful against the red canyon rock. We stood in silence, taking in the day we had just survived and the payment of treasure! Then, a moment I will remember forever: "Mom, I can't believe people can think that there is no God." On her own, my nine-year-old came to the realization that there is something much greater than us, and that sometimes He makes the most wonderful gift difficult to get, too. That moment will always reinforce that the effort is worth the price.

THE CHALLENGE IS WORTH OVERCOMING

This moment reinforced why hiking is so different from other sports and how huge the payoff is. As an adult, that hike was extremely challenging. For my nine-year-old, it was the most physically challenging thing she had ever done, and at the end of it, she had this beautiful moment of clarity. Our faith, and Creation, is so important to us. As she stood at the waterfalls, she realized how good God is and how real He is. This was the payoff for her.

She and I both overcame some big fears on that trip and made some of my most favorite memories. The way the trip started is how we've come up with a lot of our trips. All the kids watch the Travel Channel, and we've started a list of "where to next" destinations. I cannot wait for the day when we are on that African safari or gazing at the northern lights in a glass igloo! Maddie's saying, that the most beautiful things to see are the hardest to reach, resonates with our whole family.

When we go on hikes now, the girls remind each other of this when they're having difficulty with something. Even recently, when we hiked to a nearby waterfall and one of them grew tired of hiking up a rock, the others reminded her that all the best gifts and treasures take the most work, and they're hidden for us to go and find. When Izzy wanted to turn around during a difficult hike in Maui, we didn't let her. She knew, in the end, it would be worth it. When we reached the destination of the hike, there was a wooden tree swing right by the waterfall, and she couldn't have been happier with her decision to keep going.

From each hike we've experienced, we carry a special memory back with us. When Brax was only three weeks old, we hiked in Yosemite. We have a picture of me nursing him as we were coming down Nevada Falls, rounding out that seven-mile hike. Between steep terrain and switchbacks, we pushed and challenged ourselves.

We recently hiked the Emerald Bay trail in Lake Tahoe with members of our church. Izzy came up with a full, brand-new song during that hike. We hiked the upper, middle, and lower pools in Zion National Park. That was when we first noticed how much the girls had grown with hiking and that there was a maturity about them. There were steep cliffs and no railings. At times, the girls ran ahead of us, and I thought they might just run right off the cliff. But since we've started hiking, they're so much more capable and aware of their surroundings.

After hiking down to the blowhole on the northern side of Maui, Charlotte realized that hiking back up in the flip-flops she had on, which had gotten wet and slippery, was going to prove difficult. One of my all-time favorite photos is of her at the top, barefoot, pointing to the sandals below. She loves to tell the story of her hike with bare feet, and it always makes me laugh.

MORE THAN A PHYSICAL EDUCATION

Visiting national parks has become one of the more exciting aspects of traveling for our daughters. We always try to find out if the location we're visiting has a national park before we leave. They provide such a good window into the history of each state, and they are the best places to stretch our legs and take in beauty.

The Junior Ranger program allows the kids to be very involved and to learn while outdoors, providing great physical education. It's inexpensive and available just about anywhere—even other countries have national parks.

The program offers so many educational resources, but our favorite are the scavenger hunts in each park, where you end up looking throughout the whole park to find items and to become an official Junior Ranger. We use this scavenger-hunt approach wherever we go now.

Using these resources available in the national parks and with the Junior Ranger program has become essential for me in facilitating the girls' education while on the go, but more importantly, it has kept them motivated to learn. As soon as they receive their age-specific ranger booklet, they're off and running, completing the requirements for getting sworn in as a Junior Ranger and receiving their badge. They love earning badges, and they're very proud of them. They talk to the park rangers like comrades: "We were at Muir Woods and we got the one-hundredth-anniversary badge, the wooden one. Have you seen it?" The rangers think they're cool. We create memories and community on each trip.

What I hope you are seeing and realizing in these stories is that with the 5-Hour School Week, we are not just participating in physical education when we set out for a hike or visit a national park. We are also not just committing our focus to the history of that park. We aim to cover several subjects within one trip or adventure. The adventure of getting a Junior Ranger badge sparks a passion for exploring outdoors (physical education), while giving the kids an opportunity to reach out to other adults to learn something (socialization) in an environment that is teaching through all the senses within several traditional topics (history, science, biology, reading, writing, etc.). And a really cool part? Aaron and I are learning so much along the way. Maybe we are relearning something from our days at a desk, but honestly, my curiosity and passion to learn is being sparked right alongside theirs.

I often think about how this program works for kids in a traditional school setting. When I was young, we went to the zoo all the time during school break. Because my mom was a science teacher, going to the zoo was like being in a science class for eight hours, which could have been really cool had I not been exhausted from the long hours I spent in school. Instead, I had no desire to learn anything from the zoo or my mom when school was out. Our daughters have a completely different attitude toward these experiences. In every city we visit, they ask if it has a zoo or aquarium. They aren't burnt out on learning things, and they wake up excited to learn something new and to meet new people.

EXPLORING ACTIVITIES AT HOME

As parents, it's important that we find what our kids are passionate about, especially in physical education. When they're engaged in an activity, they fully benefit from that time. They then improve their skills because their focus is better, and that leads to activities that become even more enjoyable. We know that as adults, we benefit from making healthy choices consistently, such as eating healthy foods and going outside. The more consistent we are with these choices, the more quickly they become healthy habits. The same thinking applies to our kids, and it's our job to teach them those habits and provide those opportunities and experiences.

Maddie has picked up skateboarding, which she loves now after regularly practicing. Charlotte and Izzy love ropes courses because they are risk-takers and love a challenge, constantly pushing to go higher than they have before. We let them guide us in selecting activities to support them. The more time you spend with your kids to get to know them deeply, the more you'll recognize what pushes them outside their comfort zone.

FINDING NEW PASSIONS

In Hawaii, we learned to paddle-board and absolutely loved it! Coming back home, we found paddle-boarding opportunities on our local lake and river. Allow yourself to be physically inspired or possibly find a great new hobby.

At a family event recently, we had to complete a series of obstacles as a family and, along the way, collect golf balls. The competition was to get the golf balls before the other families who were competing. A section of the obstacle course involved canoeing on a river to get to the golf balls. Izzy had never been in a canoe, and before she even climbed in she decided she hated it. If she had stepped out into the water, it would only have reached to about her knees, yet my girl who loves a good adrenaline rush was terrified the entire time and couldn't explain why.

Since then, we've been on boats, and she's expressed similar feelings. Izzy just doesn't like boats and open water. It's a fear she attempts to overcome every chance she gets. We talk about that canoe trip a lot. We use it as a reminder that she survived, and then she feels brave. We talk about the fact that it's okay to be afraid, but it's important not to let that fear stop you.

BEYOND THE PLAYGROUND

This process became so much easier for us when we took the girls out of school. After a full day at school, they simply didn't have the energy to do anything. Part of the energy they have now comes not only from the freedom they have in selecting what they're going to do with their day but also from not being exhausted from sitting at a desk inside for eight hours. They choose to go outside, whereas before, it felt like a chore for me to get them out the door.

Understandably, there are limitations on the freedoms allowed to students in a traditional school setting. Liability and time restrictions keep teachers from offering students the opportunities we can offer our kids. For instance, there were two solid months this year when our girls basically lived on roller skates. They loved it, and we loved that they loved it—they were outside for hours every day, exercising and learning coordination. That just can't happen at school.

It's also difficult to line up when kids will be motivated for an activity with the strict schedule of a school day. What if they don't feel like exercising during PE or recess? They won't benefit from the class or playtime, yet they'll be pushed to be active and do well. In homeschooling, when our kids feel motivated to play outside, they play outside. We never have to motivate them to be active, and they don't develop negative associations with physical activity.

CREATING OPPORTUNITY

Although we rarely feel the need to motivate our kids to be active, we make sure that they have ample opportunities to learn new things and push themselves. We've started exploring caves, known as reverse hiking, where we hike down into deep caves in places such as Texas and Oregon. Not only is this activity physically challenging, but it is packed full of learning.

When our kids want to go outside and play for two hours, I encourage that. I prefer they play physically outside than sit and do workbooks inside. By choosing to play outside, they're creating a habit of being adventurous, getting fresh air, and making healthy choices.

They feel the benefits of making healthy choices, too. When it's hot in the summer months here in Sacramento, they can't go outside as much. The girls notice that not being able to exercise outside makes them feel more tired, that they don't have as much energy. They have a self-awareness about how they feel and move toward finding solutions to elevate their feelings—a freedom that just isn't possible in traditional school. I love finding them on their yoga mats during the summer months especially—Maddie instructing her sisters through some basic movements to stretch and get the blood flowing.

This freedom flows into every aspect of our lives, especially when it comes to health. Even the simple task of eating happens when we are hungry, instead of when it is scheduled. There is no rush to inhale our lunch to get that fifteen minutes of recess—a very important subject.

TEAM SPORTS AT HOME AND AT SCHOOL

Here are a few other comments I hear a lot: "I really want to homeschool, but my son loves baseball" or "Homeschooling would be great for us, but my daughter has tons of talent on the soccer field." The great news is that homeschoolers of all ages have the same opportunities as kids in school. Many public schools allow homeschoolers to try out for their public school district (usually determined by home address). Simply call the school and ask for their policies. On top of that, the number of city and private teams is continuously growing. Obviously, they vary from place to place, but with a little research, I guarantee there is a team for your kid.

Team sports are such an important part of our kids'

development. Aaron coaches soccer, and all three of our daughters are on soccer teams. We take three months every year to commit to soccer so that our kids are exposed to the benefits of team sports, such as learning to work together to accomplish a goal. We aren't involved in year-long leagues because, for us, the girls need the freedom—in choice and time—to be able to pursue all their interests.

Our 5-Hour School Week has made every aspect of life more enjoyable—especially soccer. This year, I'm looking forward to soccer season because I no longer have to pick the girls up from school, then rush to eat dinner in the seven-minute car ride to practice, as we used to. Back then, I'd know right away, when I picked them up from school, whether they would have a good or bad day at soccer. On the bad days, they were tired, had no energy, and often sat out practice on the sidelines. We started to wonder why they were playing soccer in the first place.

With the kids learning at home now, they finish their studies in the morning, then feel rested—and stress-free enough—to enjoy soccer later in the day. They're passionate about the game, and they enjoy spending time and learning with their teammates.

With so many benefits to gain from team sports, home-schooling families shouldn't assume it's a world they can't join because they aren't part of a traditional school. In fact, as of the writing of this book, there are ten US states that force public schools to allow homeschoolers to participate on their sports teams, and many other states have schools that have made this choice. If you are lucky enough to live in Arizona, Colorado, Florida, Idaho, Iowa, Maine, North Dakota, Oregon, Utah, or Washington, you can rest easy. For the rest of us, we can find the opportunities available by searching the local chamber of commerce website, or any city-affiliated websites, for sports programs available and calling local schools.

THE BENEFITS OF PHYSICAL EDUCATION/ ACTIVITY

I never realized how important it is for our kids to be comfortable in all that is involved in being active outdoors. They find themselves facing fears they never knew they had, challenging themselves physically and emotionally, and learning so much about themselves and the world around them.

UNEXPECTED CONFIDENCE

Our daughters were fearful of the outdoors. They didn't like feeling uncomfortable with all the stereotypical reasons people avoid going outside, such as the possibility of bears or snakes, or the likelihood of encountering a new situation that pushed them too much.

Once we started camping and hiking, they overcame all their fears. The exposure allowed them to be more adventurous and to take more risks. They've built so much confidence from conquering these fears. When your ability is never tested, it's hard to know that you can, in fact, do something with enough courage and determination.

They still feel anxious when we explore caves or go canoeing, but the struggle is always worth it to them in the end. Charlotte still cries and doubts herself when she's working on the ropes courses, but when she finishes, she radiates a joy and confidence that would be hard to emulate in any other experience.

DIG IN DEEP

For those experiencing these adventures for the first time, joining an organized group will have its benefits. In these groups, you can learn from everyone else, and especially from the guide. There are all sorts of guides available, from guided city tours to guided hikes. The first time I hiked Havasu Falls, I went with a guide. Now I feel comfortable enough with all the parts of the journey that the next time I go, it will be without a guide. There's no shame in asking for help where you need it, especially if it allows you to build your confidence and turn the experience into a healthy habit. Even more incredible and impactful are the moments your kids see you overcome challenges along the way. When I'm obviously scared or uncomfortable, not only do my kids become my cheerleaders, but they also see their mom as just another human trying to overcome something difficult. It evens the playing field, making them feel at ease about being honest and open with me.

One of our family's mottos that we apply to everything is "Dig in deep and embrace the uncomfortable." When we planned our trip to New York City, I was a bit hesitant because I thought that the size of the city, combined with all the people, the atmosphere, and the energy, might be too overwhelming for our kids. In the past, it would have been. They used to be the kids who would melt down in public. Yet, when we got there, I was surprised that we had to hold them back so they didn't get away from us. They're comfortable now living a big life, full of challenges. They embrace situations they never did in the past, and they're grateful for the opportunity to struggle, because they always know that the good lessons come from that struggle.

The physical endurance necessary to walk through all the sites in the big cities we visit is a challenge for the girls, too—and it's not necessarily their favorite challenge.

Once we get into the city and set out to explore things that interest them, such as the museums and parks, they start to fully enjoy all the physical effort they put forth to see the things they want to see. They have more energy and stamina to explore these big cities now than when we first started traveling.

DISTRACTING AND BUILDING

When you start a new lifestyle as a family, there are always challenges in the transitions. It's important for Aaron and me to remember that even though our kids have grown so much in every way since we started homeschooling, they're still kids. They have times when they're tired or cranky, or times when they don't get along—which was the case during one recent trip to Hawaii.

The best way to remedy bickering kids is to get them outside and explore. When they're challenged together, they bond to overcome obstacles and get through the situation—and often, like magic, the fighting stops.

We were at the Garden of Eden, a botanical garden on the Road to Hana, when I thought the situation with the girls could *not* get worse. The entire car ride, we listened to their fighting and complaining in the back seat. When we arrived at the trail, we noticed a huge tree that a bunch of teenagers were climbing. When the teens ran off, the girls decided they were going to climb that tree.

There's no way they're going to get up there, I remember thinking to myself. They simply weren't big enough. They stood at the base of the tree; then, by forming a sort of human chain, they hoisted one another up until Izzy was the last link at the top.

The fighting stopped. The girls were so proud that they had accomplished this together, without our help, that they forgot they were upset with one another. We finished walking around the garden for the next hour, and it was then that I felt like the trip had finally begun. We found the reset button!

Especially in homeschooling, team building within your own family is crucial. It's easy to forget, but pushing the limits physically, on a team or in a group, teaches kids how to work together and solve problems, whether that team setting be organized sports or among your own family.

TIDBITS AND TAKEAWAYS

- Find a physical activity you can do or learn to do as a family. For us, that activity is obviously hiking.
- Focus on the activities that excite you and excite your kids. That enthusiasm will motivate your family to grow their skills and enjoy building healthy habits.
- Remember that physical education has the potential to teach important life lessons, build endurance and perseverance, and have the added bonus of incorporating traditional academia into the learning environment.
- Exploring new opportunities and activities will bring out feelings, fears, and skills within your family that you may not have known existed. Those are learning moments. Remember that it's okay to be afraid or uncomfortable, but it's not okay to let it stop you.
- Homeschoolers can join public school teams in many areas, and there are several opportunities that can be explored when it comes to team sports. Start Googling. I know you can find a satisfactory solution.

GIVING YOUR CHILDREN LIFE SKILLS AND A REAL-WORLD EDUCATION

The only way to do great work is to do what you love.

—STEVE JOBS

We gained more than just time when we decided to adopt the 5-Hour School Week—we gained the freedom to teach a more well-rounded education that includes life skills and real-world elements. We have the opportunity to fill in the gaps that kids in school are missing out on, which begins when children recognize what they love and what comes naturally. They won't find that sitting at a desk! The only way to discover their passions and skills is through trial and error. The sooner you help them discover these strengths, the more time they'll have for mastery and innovation.

FEARLESS ENTREPRENEURS

Throughout the year, Aaron's entrepreneur group hosts family trips. These trips provide an opportunity to teach in a real-world environment with like-minded families. We spend time building working business models, discussing the growth mindset, and having breakout sessions that target topics that strengthen the entire family.

A NEW KIND OF SHARING

During one of these family events, we all got together to ski and spend the weekend masterminding in Whistler. We set up a two-day class for the kids to learn how to start a business and gave them the opportunity to build a working model and earn money. We prepurchased event and ski supplies such as logo backpacks and T-shirts, ski scarves, sunblock, and lip balm. We also taught them about profit and loss. First, we explained the cost of the items so they could price them for sale. Then, they were allowed to determine the amount of profit each item could bring in and given an opportunity to come up with a marketing plan. We reviewed sales and marketing strategies, advertising, and point of sale practices. We taught them about investor partnerships and the importance of giving back. The cost of goods plus a percentage would be paid to the adults for their contribution in buying products, providing sales space, and coaching. Along with those elements, a donation from their profits would go to a nonprofit.

The kids ran a pop-up store that would be open during breaks in the conference. They practiced their sales techniques. They learned how to handle products that didn't sell and had to be creative to move these. The sunscreen, for instance, didn't sell because it was overpriced; the kids decided that they could include it for free in purchases over a certain price point to encourage customers to spend more on the profitable items they liked. The kids noticed quickly which items were most popular and raised the prices (supply and demand).

During the event, they had the opportunity to practice selling products to one another, learning more and more about the items they were selling and how to sell them. We tapped into all the entrepreneurial experience we had available in the room, which gave the kids an opportunity to learn different sales techniques from professionals. They learned what to say and how to say it. They discussed questions: Is it best to allow the customer to come to you or to seek out their business by going to them? What do you say when you approach a new customer?

Over four days, they sold fifty bracelets, twenty lip balm, forty neck gaiters, twenty backpacks, and forty Hawaiian shirts, and they sold five units of sunblock and gave away twenty-five.

NOT YOUR AVERAGE LEMONADE STAND

This interactive model helped the kids learn real-world financial sales vocabulary:

Gross Revenue. Total amount of money collected: $3,742

Liquidation Sales. Dropping sales prices in order to make sure all goods are sold within the time period.

Cost of Goods Sold. Amount we paid for the supplies ahead of time: $1,925

Gross Profit. Total money collected minus total cost: $1,872

Cost of Interest/Investor. 10 percent of profit: $187

Goodwill/Donations. Donated 20 percent of earnings to nonprofit, 1 Life Fully Lived

Net Profit. All money left over before distributing to shareholders: $1,272

Share Distribution. $1,272 divided among ten kids: $127 for each kid

Obviously, not your average lemonade stand! Now everything has the potential to become a business, and the kids are able to carry what they learned on that trip as a model for any project. Homemade slime, eggs from our chicken, or travel activity binders—the girls understand the steps in building a business and the difference between cost and profit.

BUILDING AND LEARNING TOGETHER

Learning the ins and outs of a working business model and marketing strategies and experiencing the monetary reward of hard work is more impactful and educational than any amount of time spent at a desk. Building entrepreneurial-based thinking in everyday activities strengthens the thought process so kids can be solution-seeking and innovative, instead of just following instructions. For example, when I start to hear "I'm bored!" I love to have them build something "that can change the world" with their Legos or clay and then have them pitch me their idea. Projects like this cure the boredom and bring forward the creativity and outside-the-box thinking I want them to always carry, no matter where the future takes them.

Our kids can literally turn anything into a business-making moment.

Our skiing event sparked interest in the girls to learn as much as they can about profit, earning, and reselling. It also allowed us opportunities to teach them that 95 percent of new businesses fail—Aaron and I started eight businesses before one became successful.[4] Kids have a big advantage over adults when starting businesses, however, because they lack the fear of failure that holds many adults back.

One of Aaron's favorite stories about this comes from a nonprofit event that we attended in Philadelphia. Jeff Hoffman, the billionaire who invented Priceline, also attended the event, and kids were challenging each other to sell him a barrel of monkeys. One parent finally said, "If you sell that toy to Jeff Hoffman, then I'll buy one, too." The

---

4   Pek Pongpeit, "Why Do 95% of Businesses Fail within Five Years?" Quora.com, September 24, 2017, https://www.quora.com/Why-do-95-of-businesses-fail-within-five-years; Neil Patel, "90% of Startups Fail: Here's What You Need to Know about the 10%," *Forbes,* January 16, 2015, https://www.forbes.com/sites/neilpatel/2015/01/16/90-of-startups-will-fail-heres-what-you-need-to-know-about-the-10/#5b5ccc666679.

kids walked up to Jeff, talked to him about their product, and in the end, sold him a ten-dollar barrel of monkeys.

Nine out of ten times a product is pitched, customers will reject it—but one of the ten customers will be interested, and that's all you need. The sooner kids learn how to approach customers and handle both failure and success, the better salespeople they will be in their adult lives. Aaron still talks about struggling with cold-calling and with approaching strangers with his ideas. Had he practiced this skill when he was young, this would be far less of a struggle for him now.

TEACHING YOUR CHILDREN LIFE SKILLS

Children learn a lot simply by watching their parents and family. They see how we handle difficult situations, how we manage our time, and how we use money. These situations invite questions and curiosity. They're opportunities for teaching and learning. Simple tasks that seem routine to parents may be a world of mystery for their kids. We've found that involving our girls in our daily tasks and in our work has helped them find new areas they enjoy and explore new opportunities.

DRAW ON YOUR OWN SKILLSETS

Around the same time that Charlotte was born—six weeks

early—Aaron left the company where he was working and started his own real estate business. I got my real estate license and sold the homes Aaron purchased and renovated. Maddie was just two when she helped me with every step of the selling process, from walking through the home to make sure it was vacant, to marking off the checklist to note what the home needed, to listing the property. Eventually, all the girls learned the ropes and can walk into a house and notice if we will need to repaint, replace granite, or upgrade the cabinets. Nine years into our business, they understand Aaron's standard for reselling a home, and because they've sat with me at open houses, they know how a house is sold as well.

During one car ride, Aaron and I talked about a house we were selling that didn't close. Listening to our conversation, Charlotte asked, "When you buy a house, who pays for that house?" When we explained that we request a loan from a bank, she then asked about how the loan process works. By the end of that one-hour car ride, we had explained how people buy and sell houses, and who gets paid for each part of the process. Just walking our kids through the steps of purchasing a home forced us to look at the specifics in the process and understand how we're handling the business.

We encourage our kids to ask questions about our work, and they learn by completing simple tasks related to our businesses. Friends of ours practice this very thing with their children: when the mail arrives, they have their kids open it, sort the junk from the invoices, and organize it into folders. The kids are responsible for putting checks in envelopes before they mail them, and in doing so, they learn about the process of receiving and paying bills.

Another set of our friends have purchased homes with their older children as partners in their rental properties. The kids invested their savings alongside their parents. Every month, they have family business meetings to discuss income, expenses, pros and cons of owning investment properties, and what further investments they will be making. When deciding to hold on to the property or sell it, the kids have an equal vote. Similarly, they have tested investing in the stock market and hard money lending as other avenues of recurring revenue.

Our kids occasionally work with our in-house designer to learn about developing logos. The kids vote on new logo designs for the company, and Maddie has even worked with our designer to develop six different logos for her greeting card company.

The more we've been able to share with our kids, the better all our lives have become. While the lessons they learn from watching and participating are important, the family bonding moments that come from our work are equally valuable because our businesses are very much part of their lives, too, and I think we have several friends who would agree.

NEGOTIATIONS AND FAMILY DECISIONS

Our kids experience the freedom and luxuries that having entrepreneurial parents can bring. But they also understand and experience the stress of making hard choices and the importance of being willing to take actions other people won't.

Last year, as our trip to Texas was coming to an end, Aaron received notice on a deal he had been working on in Jackson, Mississippi. It was one of those "once in a lifetime" deals, and he had twenty-four hours to make a decision. This decision had the potential of changing the course of our family, so we put it to a family vote. Do we endure a crazy car trip from Dallas to Mississippi to view the property so Dad can make the decision he needs to make? It wasn't going to be a particularly fun trip, and we had already been away from home for a while. We were supposed to fly home in less than forty-eight hours and had planned on hanging at the hotel pool and getting a little R&R after a crazy week experiencing rodeos, river walks, and swimming holes. We traded in a relaxing end to that trip and went on the insanely long car ride. The property—an abandoned apartment complex in the heart of Jackson—was something straight out of a horror movie, with alligators in the overgrown swamp that now overtook the property! It was seriously a site like I'd never seen!

What an educational adventure it turned into! After jumping the seven-foot chain-link fence with all four kids, we carefully walked around the 150-unit property. We spent nearly an hour talking about the work that would need to be done before it would be habitable again. We used math to determine how many AC units and windows we thought would be needed and the projected cost. Aaron asked the girls where he should start. "Landscaping!" they all yelled in unison. Walking around waist-deep weeds with slithering water moccasins and God only knows what else was enough of an education to know that hiring a brave landscaper was to-do item number one. We talked about the tenants who would live there and our dream to create a beautiful community for them to call home. The kids were so engaged and excited for this opportunity their dad had been given, and we were so excited they were getting their first lesson in healthy risk-taking.

We ended up making that purchase, and we talked about the sacrifice and insanity of those twenty-four hours often. On the drive home, we stopped and ate gumbo in Louisiana and drove through the historic district in downtown Jackson—which crossed two more off our list of states to visit.

This Mississippi project took on a life of its own once we realized the need for low-income housing in that community. Originally, it was purchased solely as an investment opportunity, but it has now become a project of service and compassion. The girls are watching as their dad works with the city to create housing for those in need—a lengthy and complicated process. We get to talk about remaining flexible to change not only in life but also in business. That sometimes you start out thinking a deal will be for one purpose, but it morphs into something completely different, often something better.

We talk about this adventure more than any other from that trip. Not because it was the most fun day, but because we have built a beautiful dream around this property while learning some crucial life lessons! We had the opportunity to participate in a big part of Aaron's business, and we loved every moment.

INVITE THEIR CURIOSITY

Unfortunately, many kids have no idea what their parents do for a living. We believe kids should know where money comes from and how their family spends it. Our kids ask so many questions about money that I never asked when I was their age. Maddie, for instance, asked about credit cards and interest rates the other day. We had a fifteen-minute conversation about how credit cards work, the dangers of using them, and the benefits of having good credit. I compare this to where I was when I was eighteen. With three credit cards in my name and interest building, I had no idea that there was a cost to using these cards and that just making the minimum payment would not actually pay it down!

As a kid, my family rarely discussed money beyond the fact that if I wanted stuff, I needed to earn it. I think there is a huge disadvantage to kids not understanding the difference in cost and value, or how loans and credit work. I was never introduced to the principle of investing or such concepts as horizontal income. That's why Aaron and I not only talk about money in front of our kids; we talk to our kids about how it works, how it can be earned and borrowed, as well as the dangers and rewards.

Recently, the girls and I watched a documentary about the Revolutionary War. During that time, there was no formal schooling—girls learned how to read at home when they turned ten, and boys simply started an apprenticeship in place of school. Maddie wondered why kids today don't do apprenticeships and instead sit in classrooms. The sad reality is, we couldn't be any further away from the days of encouraging strong work ethic with actual work and responsibility. It seems that as a society, we are so preoccupied with a formal education in the classroom that we no longer worry about how our kids will work in the real world after their education is "finished."

REAL-WORLD SKILLS OVER CLASSROOM LEARNING

When I graduated high school, I had zero idea what my passion was or how to even find it. I had an ideology that college was the only option for success. Even though I didn't have a major or even an idea of my real passion, I was assured that there were two solid years of core classes (more math, writing, history, etc.) before I would even need to declare a major. Needless to say, I jumped in and out of community college, racking up a decent amount in student loans, and never gaining any knowledge about finding my passion or purpose.

I want more for our kids. I want them to learn the subjects, topics, skills, and information that will actually be applicable, inspirational, and valuable to their passions and purpose.

FOLLOWING THEIR PASSION LEADS TO NEW SKILLS

A few years ago, Maddie's dream was to be a baker. This career choice was based solely on her love of the Food Network and the fact that she was able to bake cookies. She wasn't passionate about baking, and she hadn't learned anything in school that motivated her toward this path. It was simply a career choice she could throw out when people asked, "So what do you want to be when you grow up?" Given the opportunity to sell her baked goods, the joy of baking drastically changed, and she realized that while she may absolutely love being in the kitchen, that might not be an actual career choice for her.

A few years later, with time and freedom to explore different paths, she's discovered that she loves building websites and coding. She's fascinated with marketing techniques and spends time working on a travel-binder company she is in the early stages of building. The girls love public speaking, and I love their ability to pitch an idea. I'm always reminded of interviews with the most successful people; they almost always talk about the "hustle" and the "grit." I feel like my girls are already working on the hustle, so we may just be going in the right direction!

SKILL NEEDS IN THE WORLD ARE CHANGING

Many skills that are taught in a traditional school environment, such as the value of memorization, are just not as valuable in today's market. Kids need to learn about public speaking, the value of money, risk-reward analysis, and how to price a product. They need to be exposed to a learning environment that teaches these skills so that they can start a business or become hirable one day. Employers are looking for innovative employees. They want more than someone who just follows instruction, and instead want someone who provides true value to a company.

The most recent report released by Dell Technologies, authored by the Institute for the Future, states that 85 percent of the jobs that will exist in 2030 do not exist today.

Early in this book, we mentioned our friend Jim Sheils, who was one of our first inspirations. When Jim first spoke to us at a family event, he asked this set of questions: "What were the three or four most difficult experiences you've had to overcome in this life? How did you get through them? Did what you learned in school prepare you for those events?"

We, and many others, weren't able to say that school had been part of our preparation for those moments. We summed up his education matrix in one sentence: The most important things you need to learn in life aren't taught in schools today.

At www.jimsheils.com, you can see a copy of his education matrix. He breaks down the most crucial needs of education into three categories: financial intelligence, relationship skills, and personal development. We would agree that all the examples in the matrix are crucial. For example, skills such as healthy risk-taking, handling ROI and cash flow, resolving conflicts, having healthy boundaries, overcoming rejection, using intuition, asking for help, and so on are just some of the skills we needed most when facing hard times. These skills simply aren't being taught in traditional schools. We try to make sure our curriculum covers all the topics in the education matrix and more.

DEVELOP SKILLS AT THEIR LEVEL

Regardless of age, children are capable of completing responsibilities and are eager to learn—from picking up toys, to unloading the dishes, to folding laundry. These everyday chores build a sense of accountability, provide service to their family, and are an early introduction to building work ethic. There are several resources online with great ideas on appropriate chores based on child age, if you feel unsure.

In the same way that we feel more confident after completing a challenge, our children become more certain of who they are and what they can do when encouraged to finish a difficult project or complete a chore that doesn't come easily to them. Making the bed can be seriously stressful for some little people, but with a little encouragement and a lot of patience, they will eventually do a great job and feel great about it!

THE CHALLENGE MAY NOT ALWAYS BE WELCOME, BUT IT'S WORTH IT

This is not to say that our kids will love or find passion in everything we ask them to do. We know there are times we all have to do things we don't want to do. Our kids complain just like anyone does when it comes to cleaning the bathroom or taking out the trash. I tolerate the complaints today because I know one day the reward will be a fully capable adult. We have to remember the goal, and I know how hard that is. I want to stop the clock and keep them little, too, but my ultimate goal is that they are independent and able, that they know how to find solutions and carry themselves with confidence, and that they can contribute value and remain teachable.

EMBRACE THE UNIQUENESS OF YOUR FAMILY

I often forget that we don't look like an average family. We ask a lot of our kids, and we expose them to a lot of stuff many parents are uncomfortable with. We talk to our kids about everything, and Aaron and I are painfully honest with them about how we spend our money, disagreements, how we feel about the other relationships in our lives, illnesses in the family, and so on. I know a lot of parents feel it's our job to "protect" kids from such topics, but with appropriate delivery and context, the rewards for being open and forthcoming with your kids will be limitless.

I'm sure some of you are going to raise your eyebrows and shake your head at this, but here is what I can absolutely testify to: our kids don't question our truthfulness, and they are aware that we will not just tell them what they want to hear. Because I am transparent with my kids, they too are an open book. They see me fail and see my vulnerability, so they are allowed to fail and be vulnerable. This is a new belief system for me. I have a lifetime of experience that taught the exact opposite, and I constantly need to remind myself that if I want openness, I must model being open.

It is when kids stop feeling comfortable asking questions that they run into the most trouble. Personally and in business, it's important that we keep curiosity alive and well and encourage questions and thought-provoking conversations. I once read, "If you won't listen to all the little stuff your kids have to share, they won't share with you the big stuff when it happens." Cultivate a relationship of communication early in life, and when the topics get more challenging, these difficult conversations will come easier.

It's obvious to our kids that the life we live is different than those of other kids, and it can be challenging to avoid comparisons or the critical eyes of others. I've heard the girls refer to themselves as the "weird" kids when going to playdates and parties for friends from our years at school. And while they feel different, they also acknowledge and appreciate the differences. Often, they will comment on the lack of freedom their friends have or how stressed out they are about homework or the lack of time they have to play.

We check in regularly: Are we still happy with this life? Is it still working? Is there a desire to find an alternative educational environment? When I started the 5-Hour School Week, it was with the understanding that we would keep going as long as we were happy and still learning. The passion for this life seems to only grow over time. There will always be a learning curve. It's a constant process of trial and error to figure out what is working and what we actually don't need. There is a process of "unlearning," because not everything we brought into this lifestyle promotes our new values. It is never about perfection or having all the answers. In fact, it's about being incredibly messy and figuring it out together.

TIDBITS AND TAKEAWAYS

- There are a lot of benefits to educating kids in business and money matters. They need to learn practical, real-world skills that will lead them in successful lives.

- There are endless opportunities in our everyday lives to help instill work ethic and promote being business-minded. Bringing your kids into your professional world will teach responsibility and learnability.

- Open and honest parents will be rewarded with open and honest kids. Build those relationships now so they're in place when it really matters.

- Focusing on applicable, purposeful, driven projects—especially those that provide value—will have far greater impact than anything learned in a book or while sitting behind a desk.

HOW TO MAKE TRAVEL AN ESSENTIAL PART OF YOUR CHILDREN'S LEARNING

The biggest adventure you can ever take is to live the life of your dreams.

—OPRAH WINFREY

By now, I'm sure you've caught on that for us, travel is not only one of the most fabulous perks of not being in school, but it's also a main tool in educating.

Between having the opportunity to travel with Aaron on business and having the flexible schedules we've built into our lives, I am able to teach all around the world! I truly believe in and am witnessing the amazing impact travel can have on kids. I swear, traveling with kids isn't as hard as you or someone else has convinced you it is.

Traveling allows us to combine into various lessons and experiences adventure, exercise, nature, culture, history, science, and the list can go on. Location only broadens your opportunities: from tasting local cuisine—such as Philly cheesesteaks in Philadelphia, deep-dish pizza in Chicago, and fish and chips in London—to exploring zoos and botanical gardens in countries such as Canada and the United Kingdom, the curriculum will build itself.

There is not a place in the world you can't spend some time researching to find its best locations, restaurants, and famous adventures—in literally minutes—thanks to Google, Pinterest, Instagram, travel blogs, and any other websites that offer travel tips. I easily plan our itinerary around the educational sites our trip's destination can offer. For example, when we found out we were going to Massachusetts, I had a blast organizing stops at the Boston Tea Party Museum, mapping out the Freedom Trail walk, and planning a day in Plymouth to experience life as a true pilgrim. We decide how immersed we want to become and what we want to learn.

IMMERSED IN EDUCATION

Choosing Airbnbs over hotels when we travel has enabled our family to make traveling a big part of our lives. Not only are Airbnbs typically more affordable, but they are perfect for families because they provide more space overall, include a kitchen area, and can be far more comfortable.

Traveling has its moments when we need to unwind after a long day of exploring. Having a homelike setting allows us to have a heightened level of calm and relaxation. On those days that we decide to stay in, I have the ability to set up the buffet of learning and give the kids a regular daily routine wherever we are.

We choose properties centrally located to give us an experience that feels the most authentic. Opting to travel like this offers us a passageway to places around the world, allowing us to see life and cultures outside our own experiences. We see what homes in the area look like, we attend their churches, and our kids make friends with the neighborhood kids. We're able to immerse ourselves more easily and more comfortably.

DIGGING INTO CULTURES

Cuba provided us the best example of how staying at an Airbnb can truly enrich our experience. We didn't feel like we were staying at a resort—and that was exactly what we wanted. Our mattresses were on the floor, and water was a luxury, so showering and even flushing the toilets were to be done sparingly.

In London, the Tube and bus stops were two blocks from our flat located above a small coffee shop. Within minutes we could be on a double-decker bus, on our way to visit one of the grand palaces in the area.

GO PREPARED

Take a lot of the stress out of travel by using convenient and helpful apps, such as Google Translate, to jump through language barriers. Look into alternative lodging options, such as Airbnb, for centrally located, economical, local-living, like-home places to stay. Then dive into the culture through food. Yelp is great to find popular and local eats.

It's important to play an active role in these types of trips. We don't sit back and wait for something great to happen to us because we are on "vacation." No, we jump in, ready to experience a new way of life as we attempt to understand and learn.

The preparation for the trip to Cuba was more focused on culture and their way of life, rather than the actual history of this complex country, as we quickly learned this would save us from confusion and significant worry. I had read, before going, that it was not uncommon for complete strangers to be overly friendly to children in Cuba. It was common for strangers to pat children on the head, offer small gifts, and speak openly to them. We would walk into a restaurant, and a waitress would scoop Brax right out of my arms. They would take the kids back to the kitchen and give them pieces of bread and small snacks while we ate. Luckily, I was semi-prepared for the extra attention paid to our kids and had prepared them as well.

Instead of shying away from local traditions, we try to embrace and practice them. Immersing ourselves in an environment completely different from our own is literally the best lesson I've been able to give our kids. Understanding how people live—around the world—is shaping their perspective in ways that are impossible to teach from a classroom.

EXPERIENCING LANGUAGE

The biggest cultural difference, in traveling to the majority of foreign countries, is typically the language. My two years of high school French was of zero help while in Cuba. And while Aaron did take a few years of Spanish, he retained very little. Avoiding the "touristy" resorts, we met very few English speakers and were fish out of water in our attempts to communicate. Luckily, Aaron had had enough forethought to download the Google Translate app. It would accurately translate a typed English phrase into Spanish.

We were incredibly surprised when we heard "Hola," as the door to our Airbnb opened early our first morning. We hadn't realized that every morning a lady would come and prepare breakfast for us—a lovely assortment of fruits, eggs, and pastries, along with coffee, milk, and juice. This sweet lady who made our meals spoke absolute zero English, and it became our favorite time of the day. Using Google Translate, we would learn Spanish while we taught our new friend English. Starting every morning this way had a huge impact on how quickly we began picking up the language.

After our yummy and educational breakfast, we would pile into the Airbnb owner's brother's tiny two-door Russian car. With no seat belts or room for a car seat, Brax would sit on my lap, and Aaron would sit in the front. Manuel was the nicest man and spoke just enough English to get us where we needed to go. He would drive us to museums, the local village for fun shops, and great restaurants. One night, he even picked us up to take us to a cannon show, where live cannons were fired out into the ocean to demonstrate how Cuba protected itself in past wars. He truly gave us the most authentic experience, which was exactly what I had hoped for.

The cultural nuances made the trip an interesting learning experience for all of us. When Maddie wanted to buy a coconut from a street vendor, for instance, we gave her the money and had her negotiate by herself. We were proud that our ten-year-old was able to take the money, talk to the vendor in Spanish, discuss the price, and purchase the coconut with no assistance from us.

EMBRACING THE UNCOMFORTABLE

When we started this educational journey and made the decision to pull the girls out of school, we hoped they would appreciate what they have and understand more about how others live. Our Cuba trip showed us that we were able to accomplish these goals with a world-school approach. It was helpful, however, that this was not our first trip. We were able to push the girls outside their comfort zone so we could all have the immersive experience we wanted for them.

This trip was successful because our daughters had learned to embrace being uncomfortable, a life skill that I could never teach at home. There were times when they were nervous, and times when they cried—they didn't know what people were saying to them, the food was completely different, and the house was not what they were used to. What they did know was that the Cubans were nice and helpful, and so they learned how to embrace the challenges of the situation.

We tried to explain how the government in Cuba was the polar opposite of that in the United States, but it wasn't until we were there, talking to the owner of the Airbnb, that the girls understood those differences and got a taste of what communism meant.

Aaron had gone to the airport to pick up our lost luggage, and our Airbnb owner came over to make sure we had everything we needed. She spoke some English, and as we began talking to her, we learned that she needed to collect our passport numbers so she could report to the Cuban government that we were staying there and how much we were paying for the Airbnb. Every dollar had to be reported because a certain percentage is paid to the government, she explained to the girls. Maddie wondered what happens if you start your own business in Cuba. "We're not allowed to start our own business," the owner replied. "The government watches everything we do, and we have to report it all to them."

Maddie thought this was completely unfair. She had never realized that being an entrepreneur is actually a freedom. This experience made it very clear to her, and to the rest of the girls, how the United States is different and what our freedom means.

Some subjects, like communism, for instance, are difficult to teach. Each trip teaches us a different way to approach the learning process with our kids. Sometimes, we research and learn everything about a place before we visit; other times, it's more beneficial to experience the place, then return home and see what kinds of questions our kids have.

LEARNING ON THE GO

To prepare for trips, I use every resource available to us, from books and worksheets to documentaries and online tutorials. Many of the worksheets we use ask the girls to complete a writing summary to capture what they've learned so far. I like to utilize what sticks with the girls most, and documentaries have been one of our most powerful teaching tools. We follow the documentaries with a short writing assignment to summarize what they've watched, and they are able to pull from this learned knowledge when we visit the landmarks they've learned about at home.

PUTTING LIFE IN THE PAGES

One morning, while staying in Boston, Maddie found herself bored as she waited for everyone to get ready, so I asked her to find some fast facts about local places to visit that she could share with her sisters. By the time I'd finished with my shower, I found the girls huddled around the computer, learning about the Boston Tea Party. We followed this up with a visit to the very hands-on, interactive Boston Tea Party Museum. At the end of the day, a simple history lesson had become a memorable experience.

With our practice of watching documentaries and learning about the locations we're visiting before we travel, we're ready to hit the ground running when we arrive at our destination. After we visit the museums or landmarks, we talk about our experience on the ride back to the hotel or during dinner. Aaron and I are constantly looking at the ways we teach the kids and asking ourselves whether they're learning what they need to from this system. I ask the girls, "What did you love learning the most? What do you want to know more about?" We review pictures together, flipping through my Facebook page or looking through the pictures on my phone. This visual review is especially helpful to Izzy because, at six years old, she needs more repetition to remember what we've learned.

I think the element that makes this type of learning so impactful lies in the fact that it's not just a "lesson" but a memory. We usually look back on these trips and talk about them often, remembering not only the awesome family time but also all the cool things we saw and the experiences we had. Our trip to Boston was so packed with new information, even for Aaron and me, that we're still digesting everything we learned. We're currently tackling a list of documentaries that further explore the history we learned about and that will answer additional questions that came up during the trip. This further exploration happens often after trips, and I let the girls decide how long they want to continue learning about a subject—I want to make sure all their questions are answered.

At times, we'll reverse the order of our system so that we watch documentaries, read additional books, or complete follow-up assignments after our visit—especially if the local museum has an interesting documentary, or if the girls are genuinely interested in a subject.

DISCOVERING REAL VERSUS HOLLYWOOD

This reversal of our system worked well in Salem, Massachusetts. It was a trip we decided to take at the last minute, and we knew the Salem Witch Museum was one place we had to visit, even though the girls' only background about witches at the time was the Disney movie *Hocus Pocus*. While obviously not a historical reference, it made them excited to visit the museum and gave them a starting point for learning. Once back at home, we were able to pull up documentaries and learn more about the witch trials.

In another instance, we decided to look up the real-life

stories of Barnum and Bailey and their famous circus. Along with almost everyone else, we had become obsessed watching the movie *The Greatest Showman* over and over. Until we took on that task, I had no idea how valuable learning through fact-checking was. When we looked up how much truth was being told, we found out that not only does Hollywood get it completely wrong, but the *real* story is incredibly interesting.

FASCINATION IN THE FACTS

Fact-checking can be a fun and incredibly interesting way to learn a topic. After watching *The Greatest Showman* (loosely based on a true story), we had fun determining fact and fiction. In fact, the characters of Phillip and Anne are completely made up for the sake of romance. However, P. T. Barnum was nearly broke before opening the museum, and it did in fact burn to the ground. Historyvshollywood.com is a great website for more such fun facts!

When preparing for our local field trip to Alcatraz, we watched the History Channel documentary *Alcatraz: Search for the Truth*. This short documentary discussed the three prisoners who escaped from Alcatraz, as well as the island's other famous prisoners. The following day, when we went to Alcatraz, Maddie and Charlotte had a list of questions from the documentary. Most national parks have videos that you can watch while you're there, and we always make this part of our visit—this trip was no different. We watched the video, and we spent four hours walking around the prison on a sort of scavenger hunt, pointing out all the things we'd learned before the trip. The girls wanted to see everything they'd learned about for themselves. It was exciting to watch them run around, looking for the inflatable boat the prisoners used to escape, or for Al Capone's jail cell. When Maddie found the replicas of the papier-mâché masks the prisoners used as decoys, she screamed to the other girls, "Here it is!" They were so excited to *experience* everything they'd learned.

INTENTIONAL EXPLORATION VERSUS UNPLANNED EXPLORATION

I couldn't blame them for wanting to dive in. It was exciting just watching them. Then I noticed that they were the only kids running around the island, pointing out their discoveries to one another and excited about putting the story together. I realized, then, how important it is to prepare them ahead of time and to do so in a way that allows them all, from the youngest to the oldest, to connect to the experience. Maddie has a background in history that Izzy doesn't, so it's important that I make the information accessible, and beneficial, to all age levels.

Twenty years ago, this would have been an overwhelming

task. Technology today allows us to watch documentaries that are interesting to everyone and to stream countless YouTube videos packed with information. The media we watched about Alcatraz included stories from prisoners who shared what it was like living on the island. It was fascinating to the girls. Reading a textbook about Alcatraz just wouldn't have been the same.

Philadelphia was one of our first educational trips. The girls were still attending traditional school, so it was exciting for them to have a hands-on experience for the first time. We started the trip by visiting the city's fun cultural landmarks, such as the steps featured in the Rocky movies, and the Philly cheesesteak restaurants. We ate at both Geno's Steaks and Pat's King of Steaks, which have a long-standing contest for the best cheesesteak sandwiches. We walked around Little Italy, eating authentic cannoli and experiencing the sights and sounds of the neighborhood.

The open-top bus tour of Philadelphia that followed gave us a quick overview of what the city is all about. We learned that some of the railroads in the Monopoly board game are based on Philadelphia railroads, and we even passed by the Reading Railroad. Just seeing this one spot allowed the girls to connect to the experience, since they play the game at home and then saw the actual location with their own eyes.

I didn't prepare the girls in advance of this trip as much as I would on future trips, so they were excited to see the sites they did know about, such as the Liberty Bell and George Washington's house. We were able to sit in the room where George Washington handed the country over to the next president and see where Betsy Ross made the American flag.

Independence National Historical Park captured all the historical elements we were looking for. The girls had their Junior Ranger workbooks that they used to travel through the park and earn their badges. This program is great for keeping kids' interest—we spent three hours there, working on the booklet and learning new things.

Philadelphia was an important trip for us because it was our first taste of world-schooling, but it also showed us that sometimes reality is not quite what we envision. Charlotte, as a first grader, had learned about the Liberty Bell and George Washington's house, and she drew pictures of what she imagined these things to look like. But the Liberty Bell is not as big and ornate as what she drew, and George Washington's house isn't a standing house anymore. When she saw these places for herself, she burst into tears with disappointment. Normally, that's not the kind of reaction you want from your kids, but the moment provided time for us to be able to talk about what the house used to look like, and how important it was—and still is.

We prepared the girls more for our New York trip, which followed Philadelphia. Since we were visiting the Statue of Liberty and Ellis Island, we talked a lot about immigration and even watched *Island of Hope*, the documentary shown at the theater on Ellis Island. We talked about what it was like for children who immigrated to the United States, brainstorming what each of us would bring with us if that were us.

I bought a 3-D puzzle of the Statue of Liberty, and we spent time putting that together, and talking about what would be the point of our New York trip and what we wanted to learn. We talked about taking a ferry to see the statue, about how the girls could work on getting their Junior Ranger badges there, and briefly about September 11.

ALLOWING EDUCATION TO SNEAK IN WHEN IT FITS

Not every trip is educational for our family either. Some trips are just vacations, where we lie on the beach and play in the swimming pool. During our educational trips, on the other hand, we are very intentional about the lessons we want to learn and about what we want to accomplish during the trip.

Hawaii is a destination where we vacation *and* visit for its educational opportunities. It was during one of our educational visits that we learned all about volcanoes, and we focused on learning about Pearl Harbor and the history of Hawaii.

Pearl Harbor was a subject that was difficult for the girls to sit and learn about without experiencing the destination first. It was easier to spark their interest in Alcatraz before we went there, but during the week before Hawaii, the girls showed little interest in Pearl Harbor. Once we arrived, their interest grew, and I let their questions lead the rest of the lesson. I found that the *real* prep work for me, as their facilitator, was making the subject at least matter to them before we arrived. I covered the very basic ideas behind the event so that they knew there was a big war that the United States was involved in and that our country began its involvement in this war when Pearl Harbor was bombed. The girls had a lot of questions about why the bombing occurred, what the bombing meant, and why the war happened in the first place.

When we reached Pearl Harbor, they understood enough to want to learn more. They knew that this spot was important to our country's history, and they began watching the videos available and learning what they could. The girls knew that this was a somber moment, and they were respectful. They simply couldn't believe that sailors were still trapped underwater when we took the boat out to the memorial site.

INVITING NEW EXPERIENCES

Every trip has its own dynamic, and the significance of some destinations is just easier for kids to understand than that of others. While each location has its own set of challenges and benefits, we have found that the more interactive opportunities there are available, the more successful the trip.

Boston has been our most successful trip yet. From the Boston Tea Party Museum to Paul Revere's house, almost everything was an interactive experience. The Freedom Trail allowed us to see so many important American Revolution sites all by walking through downtown Boston. Charlotte was again disappointed at Plymouth Rock, but it gave us the opportunity to discuss why something so small and seemingly insignificant matters a lot. We felt like we had stepped back in time to the 1500s when we visited the Plimoth Plantation village, a replica of the first colony. Between the working gardens and farms, and the people in costume acting like the first settlers, the experience gave us a taste of that era.

There was so much history packed into our Boston trip. It was important that we didn't overwhelm the kids, either with too much information or with too many activities. We went to the Franklin Park Zoo one day, where we ate ice cream, saw animals, and played at the playground. In the middle of all our museum visits, we went to the

Boston Children's Museum and spent the whole day there. These were still great learning experiences, but they provided us all with the chance to regroup and refresh—a necessity on these educational trips.

LEARNING BECOMES PART OF US

By taking our kids to these major historical sites and letting them experience history firsthand, they see history as actual, significant moments in time. They're not sitting at a desk learning about a theory or timeline; they're seeing it for themselves. As a family, we've seen so much together—we stood where George Washington once stood, and we rode bikes through lava fields to watch an active volcano spill lava into the ocean!

I sometimes wonder which lessons are the "biggest" ones we're teaching them—these huge historic and scientific ones, or the moments when they learn how to participate in the world around them. That's the beauty of it. They are learning about flexibility and patience because, honestly, luggage gets lost and planes get missed. While we are figuring out how to maneuver transportation, we are also taking in a lesson that they would never learn at school. And the coolest part is...we get to do it with them!

TIDBITS AND TAKEAWAYS

- Traveling isn't a requirement of the 5-Hour School Week—we just love it and have found lots of benefits in taking our kids' education to different parts of the world. For those who need or want to stay close to home, there are still tons of opportunities and resources for learning. Your only limitation is your imagination.

- Travel exposes us to lifestyles, foods, and transportations that are much different than our own. Reading about another place can only go so far. Stepping foot in a space beyond home gives life to the lessons kids can learn.

- Watching documentaries before the trip will add to the educational feel. They will give your kids a head start on what they'll learn and help them dive in more quickly and dig into the information.

- Having an immersive education is typically more impactful. The lessons are learned more quickly, and overall, the material is remembered and understood. Kids have the opportunity to connect the dots and discover that they have even more questions to find answers to.

- National parks are a good first trip for experimenting with learning while traveling. They have Junior Ranger programs and activities for kids of all ages.

- Traveling has the ability to teach outside of classroom topics: patience, perseverance, the importance of remaining flexible, and the reward of pushing yourself in uncomfortable situations. Step outside your comfort zone and see what lessons you learn alongside your children.

THE LESSONS WITHIN THE LESSONS

Educating the mind without educating the heart is no education at all.

—ARISTOTLE

It's amazing the changes we've seen in the girls since we started the 5-Hour School Week. We're watching them grow and learn in ways that never would've been possible in a traditional school environment. Every family will see these changes develop differently, but here are the ways we've seen our girls learn more about themselves and the world around them.

WHAT WE SEE NOW

I see a confidence in my kids that I didn't see before. Maybe it had always been there, and maybe teachers and friends had seen it, but I had definitely been missing out. Having them home has shown me what they're passionate about and what they want to excel in—I think the flexibility they have to learn and explore has given them room to figure out what they enjoy for themselves.

Maddie, for instance, just finished a business meeting. She was FaceTiming with someone who was interested in including her in a book about entrepreneurial kids. Two years ago, she lacked the confidence to even reply "Hello" when friends of ours would introduce themselves. Fear quashes confidence. The girls are becoming more comfortable by the day, walking through situations fearlessly. Where it used to be difficult to even introduce themselves or speak to a waiter at a restaurant, now I sit back and watch our girls share stories of adventure with just about anyone who will listen.

WE'RE A TEAM

Frankly, we had no idea that we weren't meeting our full potential as a family. We used to be so exhausted by the end of a long day of work, school, and activities that never lined up. Now we're a team with common interests and time for one another.

We cheer each other on. We are present in each other's lives. I know the situations my kids are in and the passions they aspire to in a way I didn't before. We talk all the time, and we are invested in one another's success in ways that are meaningful and impactful for each of us. Even the kids cheer on Aaron and me in our endeavors. When Aaron has a particularly exciting day at auction and buys a dozen homes, the girls go wild congratulating him. They are our biggest supporters for this book, constantly talking about how cool it will be for Mom and Dad to have a book. Allowing us to work on it can be a sacrifice for them at times.

SELF-CONFIDENCE AND GROWTH

I just read an article released from Harvard titled, "What's Worth Learning in School?" What's interesting about this article is that it doesn't address a single traditional subject that is actually taught in schools. It notes such attributes as self-confidence, personal responsibility, self-awareness, and the ability to recognize and choose both happiness and kindness. While I can admit that maybe we didn't cover every chapter in the fifth-grade history book that most of her peers did in the classroom, I can easily say Maddie and her sisters have had many lessons that addressed all of the above.

There is no denying that there is great value in knowing

yourself and having the strength to remain true to who you are. Self-confidence breeds success more than any one thing that can be taught. Growing and nourishing that trait in our kids is what will set them up for a life of greatness and happiness.

It has been such a joy to watch each girl evolve with her new freedoms. I used to be so crazy opinionated about what they wore, always picking out their outfits with coordinating shoes and bows, never asking if they liked it or, more importantly, how they felt in what I'd picked out. But even giving that choice to them has been amazing. They each have such great style, and it really is all their own. They feel more comfortable and secure wearing what they choose, and it shows in the way they carry themselves.

EXPLORING UNIQUENESS

From fashion to education to communication, we are embracing being unique. Those whom we typically admire and are amazed by are those who stand out. We want our kids to embrace their own uniqueness and, in the same way, stand out—to break the mold, to be innovative. The last thing I want is for them to feel the need to "fit in" or be like someone else. We talk daily about being comfortable and confident in their own skin as part of our 5-Hour School Week.

A REAL-WORLD EDUCATION ALL AROUND US

One of my favorite parts of this whole educational adventure is being able to take current happenings in the world and add them to our curriculum. Just recently, for example, we were lucky enough to experience the first total solar eclipse that has been visible in much of North America in nearly forty years.

For the eclipse viewing, we traveled to Jackson Hole, Wyoming, and made an entire lesson-filled trip of it. We learned about the importance of that eclipse, that it was the only one like it for another ninety-nine years, and reviewed a map to see which states would be able to see it best. Once we'd spent time learning all we could, we experienced it as a family!

In Jackson Hole, we rode a chairlift to the top of a mountain and watched the eclipse from eight thousand feet up. The eclipse created a shadow over the Grand Tetons, and a sunrise and sunset that was unmatched by any we'd ever seen. We listened to an astronaut, who was also watching the eclipse, speak about his space exploration, and the girls got to meet and talk to him about being an astronaut.

Once back home, we worked on our outline for the week. Charlotte wanted to learn more about outer space and space exploration. It was interesting to see her draw inspiration from our Jackson Hole trip and multiply that moment into an entire curriculum she's now driving with her own interests. We get to learn big, important things from trips like these, but the 5-Hour School Week is not only about the big bucket-list moments. We can take the day-to-day and turn it into learning experiences as well. These are the moments that have great impact on their future adult lives.

We talk about the cost of goods at grocery stores and the difference in quality and quantity. We talk about current events during the day, as they are happening. When Texas had horrible floods last year, we talked a lot about the devastation of floods, how they impact people's lives, and the systems that are in place to help. We talk about safety in crowds after public and school shootings. We talk about how and why these things happen and how we think we can help. I refuse to shield them from these devastating events, because I believe our kids have the power to change this world. But they can't be part of the solution if they don't understand the problem. The world is our classroom, and our children need the opportunity, encouragement, and nourishment to explore and discern all that surrounds them.

THERE'S ENERGY IN LEARNING

Our girls understand that learning is our way of life. Our kids don't look forward to a time when we "don't have to learn anymore," like many kids who count down the days until they graduate. Learning isn't a chore; it's a passion and a privilege to us—something we get to apply to our lives.

There are no summer breaks in the 5-Hour School Week, and if you walk into our house on a random Saturday, you may find kids actually doing "schoolwork." I don't use a typical grading system to evaluate whether they are learning. I have felt there's a problem with the current grading system for a while, breeding unhealthy competition, expectations, and pressure. I instead evaluate the girls on understanding. We aren't learning to pass a test. We are learning so that we can improve ourselves and get better at what's important to us.

Our approach is not always innately easier. When we're getting on a plane, it takes more effort to encourage a learning moment by having them find their own seats. It's easier to pick out our kids' shoes for them or grab the milk at the grocery store myself. Before we started the 5-Hour School Week, I didn't realize how valuable these experiences were for our kids, and frankly, I was too tired to parent this way.

It wasn't until we changed our educational approach that I had the energy and time to let the kids be more independent and to supply them with the tools they needed to get there. I've learned how capable our girls are during this journey, and I've seen how valuable this process has been to our whole family—we just needed to create the right environment to let them flourish.

Part of providing this environment is giving kids more freedom than we may have had. So often, I see parents overprotecting their kids when it comes to school, or in how they interact in public, or with their media consumption. Kids today are growing up in a different world than we did, and we, as parents, need to give them the freedom to grow up in this world. We make a major mistake by trying to raise them according to the rules of our generation.

LEARNING AFTER HOMESCHOOL

We have friends who homeschooled their son and, even from an early age, allowed him to pursue his interests. When he was fourteen, he told his parents that he wanted to be a conceptual artist for the movies. It was a lofty goal for a teenager, especially when he'd demonstrated minimal drawing ability. He started with stick figures and devoted himself to learning the concepts behind drawing and art.

After community college, he attended art school and decided the pace was not fast enough for him, so he started taking master's-level classes with people working in the entertainment industry. Currently, at twenty-two, he's working as a conceptual artist at an animation studio. Our friends' son was able to make his dreams come true because he made his own unconventional educational path and stuck to it. He has no degree, but that doesn't matter for his industry—and he knew that all along, even when his parents worried about him veering away from the conventional college degree.

A 2018 article in *Glassdoor* reports fifteen "more" companies that no longer require college degrees, including powerhouse companies such as Google, Apple, and Ernst & Young. Trade schools, in response to continued education, are on the rise, as degrees cost more money to obtain and carry less value with each passing year.[5]

During his high school years, our friend's son was able to devote his time to what he truly loved in a homeschooling environment. He knew he could be good at digital art, and he was given the freedom to find the best way to achieve his goal. In a traditional high school, the environment would have been too restrictive and structured, and he would have wasted time on subjects that had no use to him. Even the regular college courses were use-

---

5   Glassdoor Team, "15 More Companies That No Longer Require a Degree—Apply Now," Glassdoor, August 14, 2018, https://www.glassdoor.com/blog/no-degree-required/.

less for his goal. However, he chose his path from an early age, was given the room to grow and explore, and accomplished something in eight years that a fourteen-year-old in a traditional educational environment might never accomplish.

5-HOUR SCHOOL WEEK AS AN INTERDISCIPLINARY LIFESTYLE

We refer to the 5-Hour School Week as an interdisciplinary model. This means that the projects our kids work on cover five or six subjects per project. While we were in Jackson Hole for the eclipse viewing, we attended our entrepreneurial conference. Instead of the kids selling products like they had in Whistler, this time they participated in a project called Fam Tank. It was a spin-off of *Shark Tank* where the kids brainstormed their own business ideas and presented them to a panel of judges, all of whom were successful adult entrepreneurs.

Maddie's business idea was an adventure binder that combined kids' favorite activities into one binder that they could take with them on trips. They were customizable according to their age, gender, where the kids were visiting, and their preferred activities. She identified a need and presented it by sharing her personal travel experience: when she travels, all her activity books take up so much room and are so heavy that they barely fit in her backpack. She told the Fam Tank that one binder with a select mixture of activities would solve this problem.

She listed the cost of her favorite activities—Mad Libs, crossword-puzzle books, Sudokus—to show the expense of buying everything separately versus buying one binder. She showed her audience of seventy people and ten judges that you could spend forty-seven dollars on a heavy, clumsy mess, or twenty-five dollars on one neat binder that captures all your needs and fits nicely in a backpack.

With this one project, she worked on marketing, profit/loss margins, public speaking, and advertising. More importantly, she drew connections from the real world to come up with her business idea. She identified a real need and found a real, successful solution. She even sold product after the presentation and made seventy-five dollars.

This all took place during a trip where we witnessed a historical eclipse and visited two amazing national parks! These are all skills she'll be able to use far beyond her "school" years. These are skills for life.

REAL SUCCESS

Business education and the value of money are rarely taught in traditional K–12 schools. While we may be a bit biased as entrepreneurs, as Aaron often points out, we are strong believers that the most important skill you can learn is how to start a business. If you can learn how to create something out of nothing, you can be prepared for whatever comes your way. Everyone dreams of happiness and security for their kids, so what better way to ensure this type of lifestyle than teaching them about entrepreneurship in addition to their interests?

This doesn't mean that everyone has to run their own business to feel secure or successful. Learning these skills allows you to add value in any work setting. Even when you work for someone else, the ability to innovatively accomplish the goals of the business in ways other employees aren't even thinking about will make you indispensable.

Your kids are never too young to have the entrepreneurial seed planted within them. Aaron and I have talked to the kids substantially about business concepts and involved them in our businesses, so the groundwork is laid. This has helped Maddie come up with her own business ideas by identifying needs, solving problems, and turning her solutions into income.

Entrepreneurship is certainly a strong focus for our family, but the real-world value of the 5-Hour School Week extends beyond business concepts. We allow our kids to cook with minimal supervision, motivated by their willingness to teach one another. They're capable, at all ages, of learning from their siblings or peers, and they're capable of being independent learners. We involve them in grocery shopping, buying airline tickets, planning subway rides, and paying taxi drivers—all of these activities provide real-world lessons. Perhaps more importantly, however, they learn to appreciate the effort put forth and the money spent in regular daily life.

WHERE WE CAN IMPROVE

Long ago, schoolhouses used to be one room where kids of all ages learned together. This allowed younger kids to see older kids as role models, both in maturity and in education. Older kids had the opportunity to teach the younger ones and build their own confidence by demonstrating that they'd mastered a subject.

The current school system restricts kids from learning beyond their age or grade level. We've already talked about how kids are so much more capable than we, as adults, think, so why limit what they can learn each year and limit their ability? If kids are capable of learning it, then we should be teaching it. One of the aspects I love most about the 5-Hour School Week is that Izzy and Charlotte are learning at the same pace in many subjects, and Maddie is teaching them many things that she's already learned. Maddie learns how to teach, and Izzy and Charlotte can learn whatever they want, with no limitations. Maddie also knows how she learned the content best, and the learning process is fresh to her. She teaches the content that stuck with her, and she's able to teach more effectively. This often makes her a better teacher to the younger kids because she can relate to their experience more easily.

Our kids' world should be the real world instead of structured around artificial boundaries. As adults in the real world, we interact with people of all ages. The social environment at school can limit what kids are capable of learning. Eighteen months ago, when she was still in school, Maddie had a hard time talking to anyone. At home, she's been able to build her confidence by teaching her siblings and practicing her presentation skills in front of them. Her sisters are a more comfortable, forgiving audience than her school peers were. She's now so comfortable with public speaking that she can present her ideas on stage, in front of a large audience of all ages, with no problem—in fact, she's great at it. It was important for us to provide her with a comfortable environment where she could grow confidently.

Kids want to learn, and they're naturally curious about everything. I remember being curious as a kid and being interested in learning, but at some point, it became a chore instead of a journey. I never wanted our kids to feel that way about education. Right now, they're so vocal about what they want to learn, and it's important we keep it that way.

NOT ENOUGH, ALWAYS ENOUGH

I worry about the pressures of this world. It feels like we are in a race all the time—to grow up faster and learn quicker. Most of our own parents didn't even start reading lessons until the first grade, at age seven. My girls were introduced to sight words in preschool, at age four. Why? Why are we in such a hurry? Seriously, kids need to be kids longer than we are allowing.

We are encouraging a feeling that whatever they do is just not enough, no matter what "it" is. Someone else is doing it earlier, better, and faster. What they hear is that they are not enough. And that is a hopeless feeling.

When Izzy was still in school and had just started kindergarten, the teacher's aide expressed real concern because Izzy only knew forty sight words at age five. She told us she should have been able to read closer to one hundred. Where do they even come up with these numbers and expectations? Why is the number the same for every kid?

If we have an entire lifetime to learn what we need to

know, but childhood is fleeting, let's let them be kids—kids who are passionate lifelong learners!

Aaron and I are teaching our kids that we take our own path. Just because something has been a certain way for a period of time does not make it right.

CHECK IN WITH YOUR VALUES

In the book *The Miracle Morning for Parents and Families*, we learned the value of practicing CHARMS every day with our kids. It's a great way to do a quick check-in to evaluate whether we're focusing on these things that are important to us:

C: Creativity

H: Health

A: Affirmations

R: Reading

M: Meditation

S: Service

Where is your family focused?

Our kids were born in a world that looks a lot different than the world I was born in. I adapted to cell phones, computers, and social media, but our kids are natives to this environment. They'll never know a time when they can't easily download something or Google an instructional video. What's new is often scary, and as parents, our inclination is to protect our kids. Rather than understanding how the resources and advances available today can benefit our kids, we tend to shelter them. We limit their screen time or try to eliminate it from their lives completely. How do you eliminate something that they need to know about? There is nothing our kids will do in the future that doesn't involve technology; their success is dependent on their ability to understand computers. I'd rather embrace the reality of their future and teach them how to use technology responsibly than deny them the opportunity of benefiting from it.

TIDBITS AND TAKEAWAYS

- Ask yourself what success means, for you and for your kids. Are you aiming for Harvard? Are you aiming for academic excellence? Are you aiming for young entrepreneurs? Or perhaps some combination of these, or something else? Before you can take on your own schooling for your children, you need to have a goal in mind based on the values you've set within your family. Those values will be your guiding light each and every day.

- Kids with confidence will become happy, successful adults. More than a college degree, employers are looking for a specific mindset and attitude when hiring. Of all the changes I've seen in our journey, this has been the most impactful.
- Interdisciplinary education allows opportunities to cover several subjects in one project or experience. This way of learning is not only more engaging and impactful, but exactly how it works outside of the classroom.
- Take every opportunity to tell your kids they are enough, that what they accomplish is enough, because the world will constantly be telling them they aren't. Be a source of encouragement they never have to doubt.
- We are learning and figuring this adventure out together. Not only are we all learning a lot about team building, but we are growing stronger as a family in the process. Having the opportunity to passionately learn alongside our kids is pretty incredible!

CONCLUSION

Homeschooling families believe in a different future for our children.

The skills kids need today to be successful in the future are so different from what their parents learned in school. The ability to research, navigate technology, and analyze the information they find is more important than learning to memorize textbooks. When I hear statistics that say that 80 percent of the jobs our kids will have in the future haven't even been invented yet, I realize how important it is that we teach our kids flexibility and the ability to adjust to a changing world.[6]

---

6   Daniel Tencer, "85% of Jobs That Will Exist in 2030 Haven't Been Invented Yet," Huffington Post, July 14, 2014, https://www.huffingtonpost.ca/amp/2017/07/14/85-of-jobs-that-will-exist-in-2030-haven-t-been-invented-yet-d_a_23030098/.

The foundation of the 5-Hour School Week was in our family's unhappiness with the life we were living. I was an exhausted mom raising exhausted kids. Now I have the best hours of the day with them—and they have me at my best. I get to see my kids learning, and that's a gift I was giving up, giving away all those years. Even while watching them struggle with a subject, I know they'll work through it and arrive at the other side, where they'll be proud and accomplished. Seeing them experience the world in this way is the biggest reward of this whole process.

Aaron always reminds me when we've had a rough day that we decided to take this journey together as a family because our kids were growing up without us and that we will never regret spending too much time with them.

There's probably a reason you bought this book. Maybe it's a feeling like I had—a constant curiosity about whether there was something more for your kids. Maybe homeschooling has been on your mind and heart for years, but it's been scary or seemingly impossible. You're tired of missing out; you want more for yourself and you want more for your kids. Maybe you are already homeschooling...and it's hard and not going the way you imagined. You're thinking of giving up, but still you believe in the value of having your kids home.

We are here for you! Let go of that fear. Let go of whatever you've allowed to hold you back. Let go and get comfortable with being uncomfortable. It may seem impossible and overwhelming at first. We were not exactly what most people would think of as homeschooling poster parents. There have been challenges and lots of lessons learned the hard way. But I promise, you are capable. I promise this is not as hard as you are telling yourself it is. If homeschooling is what you dream of, you can make it happen. Above all, it's worth it!

Take that first step outside of your comfort zone. Be brave and let go of the fear keeping you from getting the best of your kids, that fear that's keeping them from getting the best of you.

Connect with us and keep learning about the 5-Hour School Week and how we continue to work it into our lives for the benefit of our children and our family. Find ways to make it a part of your family's new adventure together.

Follow us at www.thefivehourschoolweek.com, and on Instagram and Facebook at the 5-Hour School Week. We will be constantly updating you with new adventures, projects, and curriculum, and we will even have a section to your kiddos from our kiddos. The 5-Hour School Week is about community. Let's come together to ask the questions, help, and support each other while living our best lives with our kids!

ACKNOWLEDGMENTS

Our biggest thanks and admiration go to all those who have been on this homeschool journey from the very beginning. To those who not only knew we had choices but have created more avenues and innovative curricula, we are beyond grateful and inspired. A shout-out to those who teach us to grab life big and live it in the front row— our life is fuller and more meaningful because of the impact you make on our entire family! For our greatest cheerleaders, everyone who has supported us, encouraged us, and believed in us, this book would not exist without you.

Most importantly, thank you to our children, who were willing to leave the classroom and embrace a completely different experience. It is in their bravery and determination that I find the assurance that we are on the right path for our family. Their creativity and ability to remain flexible as we figure it out motivates us daily!

ABOUT THE AUTHORS

An entrepreneur by nature, Aaron has built several successful businesses (of course, with his fair share of total fails) over the last ten years. However, his real passion is creating big memories with his family. Motivated by leaving a legacy of no regrets and instilling the importance of service and lifestyle innovation, Aaron is the leader of this crazy tribe. He stresses the importance of not taking ourselves too seriously, constantly reminding us that having fun along the way is crucial. A present and active member of the 5-Hour School Week, he teaches us to live life really big and to love unconditionally.

A recovering workaholic, Kaleena walked away from her busy real estate business to step into a role she had never imagined: building the 5-Hour School Week with her husband and four little humans. She is now on a journey of creating lifelong memories and impactful lessons and of passionately learning alongside her children. Kaleena dreams of inspiring and motivating parents and kids to live their very best life together.

INTERESTED IN MORE FROM THE 5 HOUR SCHOOL WEEK FAMILY?

Find our newest content at
FIVEHOURSCHOOLWEEK.COM/LINKS

Join our newsletter for practical advice and keeping up with the family at
FIVEHOURSCHOOLWEEK.COM

Join our Communities for Quick Tips on Instagram and Community Questions and Answers on Facebook

@5HOURSCHOOLWEEK   5 HOUR SCHOOL WEEK

Check out our Youtube page for our Series

"I WANT TO HOMESCHOOL BUT...."
PLUS TONS OF FUN FAMILY VIDEOS.

Looking for speakers or coaching?
We focus on helping people create:

- THE IDEAL FAMILY LIFESTYLE FOR THEMSELVES. (EVERYONE'S IS DIFFERENT)
- CREATING EFFICIENT, PRODUCTIVE AND SUCCESSFUL BUSINESSES THAT ALLOW FOR FLEXIBILITY
- ACCOMPLISHING GOALS AS A COUPLE AND A FAMILY
- CREATING YOUR BEST LIFE! IT IS NEVER TOO LATE!

REACH OUT TO US: KALEENA@FIVEHOURSCHOOLWEEK.COM